Understanding the Bible

A GUIDE TO READING THE SCRIPTURES

Understanding the Bible

the

A GUIDE TO READING THE SCRIPTURES

Saint Mary's Press®

The publishing team included Virginia Halbur, general editor; Brian Singer-Towns, co-editor; Jerry Ruff, college division editor; Lorraine Kilmartin, reviewer; prepress and manufacturing coordinated by the production departments of Saint Mary's Press.

Cover image royalty free from iStock

Printed in the United States of America

7017

ISBN 978-0-88489-852-8

Library of Congress Cataloging-in-Publication Data

Understanding the Bible : a guide to reading the Scriptures.

    p. cm.

ISBN 978-0-88489-852-8 (pbk.)

    1. Bible—Introductions. I. Saint Mary's Press.

BS475.3.U53 2009

220.6'1–dc22

                                                              2008030860

Acknowledgments

The quotations on pages 6, 6, 18, 13, 21, 21, and 56 are taken from *Dogmatic Constitution on Divine Revelation (Dei Verbum,* 1965), numbers 21, 10, 11, 13, 22, 13, and 19, respectively, at www.vatican.va/archive/hist_councils/ii_vatican_council/documents/vat-ii_const_19651118_dei-verbum_en.html, accessed June 26, 2008.

The quotation on page 8 is from *And God Said What?: An Introduction to Biblical Literary Forms,* revised edition, by Margaret Nutting Ralph (Mahwah, NJ: Paulist Press, 2003), page 29. Copyright © 1986, 2003 by Dr. Margaret Ralph.

The quotation on page 20 is from *The Christian Faith in the Doctrinal Documents of the Catholic Church,* number 1507, edited by J. Neuner and J. Dupuis (Westminster, MD: Christian Classics, 1975), page 71. Copyright © 1975 by Christian Classics.

The second and third quotations on page 21 and the quotations on pages 24–25 are from the Pontifical Biblical Commission's *The Interpretation of the Bible in the Church,* by Libreria Editrice Vaticana (Washington, DC: United States Conference of Catholic Bishops [USCCB], 1996), I.A.a, III.D.2.c, I.A., I.F., and I.A.a, respectively.

The final quotation on page 21 is from the Pontifical Biblical Commission's *The Jewish People and Their Sacred Scriptures in the Christian Bible,* by Libreria Editrice Vaticana, number 87, at www.vatican.va/roman_curia/congregations/cfaith/pcb_documents/rc_con_cfaith_doc_20020212_popolo-ebraico_en.html, accessed June 26, 2008. Copyright © 2002 by Libreria Editrice Vaticana.

The quotation on page 22 is from *Catholics Remember the Holocaust,* by the National Conference of Catholic Bishops (Washington, DC: USCCB, 1998), page 34. Copyright © 1998 by the USCCB.

The first quotation on page 23 is from *Declaration on the Relation of the Church to Non-Christian Religions (Nostra Aetate,* 1965), number 4, at www.vatican.va/archive/hist_councils/ii_vatican_council/documents/vat-ii_decl_19651028_nostra-aetate_en.html, accessed June 26, 2008.

The second and third quotations on page 23 are from *God's Mercy Endures Forever: Guidelines on the Presentation of Jews and Judaism in Catholic Preaching,* numbers 20 and 19, by the Bishops' Committee on the Liturgy (Washington, DC: USCCB, 1988), page 10. Copyright © 1988 by the USCCB.

Portions of the glossary are drawn and adapted from Saint Mary's Press® *Essential Bible Dictionary,* by Dr. Sheila O'Connell-Roussell (Winona, MN: Saint Mary's Press, 2005). Copyright © 2005 by Saint Mary's Press. All rights reserved.

Portions of the glossary are drawn and adapted from *What Do Catholics Mean By . . . ?:* Saint Mary's Press® *Glossary of Theological Terms,* by Rev. John T. Ford (Winona, MN: Saint Mary's Press, 2006). Copyright © 2006 by Saint Mary's Press. All rights reserved.

To view copyright terms and conditions for Internet materials cited here, log on to the home pages for the referenced Web sites.

During this book's preparation, all citations, facts, figures, names, addresses, telephone numbers, Internet URLs, and other pieces of information cited within were verified for accuracy. The authors and Saint Mary's Press staff have made every attempt to reference current and valid sources, but we cannot guarantee the content of any source, and we are not responsible for any changes that may have occurred since our verification. If you find an error in, or have a question or concern about, any of the information or sources listed within, please contact Saint Mary's Press.

Contributors

Reviewers and Coordinating Editors

Margaret Nutting Ralph, PhD
(Introductions to the Old Testament)
Director of the Master of Arts Program
for Roman Catholics
Lexington Theological Seminary
Lexington, Kentucky

Catherine Cory, PhD
(Introductions to the New Testament)
Associate Professor of Theology
University of Saint Thomas
Saint Paul, Minnesota

Authors of Articles on Reading and Studying the Bible

Martin Albl, PhD
Mary C. Boys, SNJM, PhD

Margaret Nutting Ralph, PhD
Shannon Schrein, OSF, PhD

Authors of Introductions to the Old and New Testament

James E. Brenneman, PhD
(Introduction to the Pentateuch)
President of Goshen College
Goshen, Indiana

David A. Bosworth, PhD
(Introduction to the Historical Books)
Professor of Old Testament Studies
Barry University
Miami Shores, Florida

Shannon Schrein, OSF, PhD
(Introduction to the Wisdom and Poetry
Books)
Professor and Chair of Religious Studies
Lourdes College
Sylvania, Ohio

Lisa W. Davison, PhD
(Introduction to the Prophets)
Professor of Old Testament
Lexington Theological Seminary
Lexington, Kentucky

Christopher McMahon, PhD
(Introduction to the Gospels and Acts)
Assistant Professor of Theology
University of Mary
Bismarck, North Dakota

Catherine Cory, PhD
(Introduction to the Letters and Revelation)
Associate Professor of Theology
University of Saint Thomas
Saint Paul, Minnesota

Charts

Sheila O'Connell-Roussell, DMin
Instructor of Biblical and Pastoral Theology
Marylhurst University
Lake Oswego, Oregon

Contents

Maps

Alphabetical List of Bible Books with Abbreviations Used in This Guide

Glossary of Biblical and Related Terms

Introduction

The Bible.

What comes to mind when you hear that phrase? The inspired word of God? A history of the Jewish and Christian faiths? A guide for living? A great work of literature? A dusty old book that has little relevance for the world today?

A host of other questions may surface as well. Are all Bibles the same? What's the difference between the Old and New Testaments? When was the Bible written? Who wrote it, and why? How are we to understand the Bible today?

Those are tough questions, questions that can't be answered by a handful of articles, some charts and maps, a timeline, and a glossary. The best way to begin to understand and appreciate the Bible, not surprisingly, is to read it. But to read it well, with understanding, those articles, charts, and maps, and that timeline and glossary can be extremely helpful, and so we have provided them here.

We realize that students come at the Bible from a variety of perspectives, including some with no religious or faith tradition at all. You may be reading the Bible as part of a Scripture study, or as literature, or for other academic or religious reasons. Also, many different translations of the Bible are available; we don't know which version you have. Regardless of your background, your beliefs, your questions, or the Bible translation you are reading, this guide has been created to help inform your reading and enrich your understanding of the Bible from historical, literary, and faith perspectives.

Inside are articles that explore the Bible in its faith, historical, and cultural contexts. The Bible is explored as literature too—its genres and literary forms. There are articles introducing the Old and New Testaments. The history and differences of translations are discussed, and other tools to help you unlock the Bible are introduced. Other aids are provided as well, notably maps, charts, a timeline, and a glossary. Together these further explore the Bible and the world in which it was written, as well as the progression of scholarship that helps us understand the Bible today.

We highly recommend that you treat the Bible as your primary source and use this guide to help you unlock and understand the Scriptures.

Jerry Ruff, Editorial Director
College Division
Saint Mary's Press

Reading and Studying the Bible

What Is the Bible?

Regardless of their faith background or religious beliefs, many people at some time ask themselves: "What is a Bible?" "How did the Bible come into existence?" "Why does the Bible have such authority in some people's lives?" "How does a person correctly understand what the Bible has to say?" For Christians, these questions carry added importance, as the answers to them say something about how God has revealed God's self over the centuries, as well as about God's self-revelation today. In one well-known biblical psalm, the narrator offers a prayer to God the lawmaker: "Your word is a lamp for my feet, / a light for my path" (Ps 119:105). Christians today continue to look to the Bible as that word, that lamp.

The Bible is not one book but a library of books. Whereas a book is usually all one kind of writing, a library includes a variety: myth, legend, history, biography, and fiction, to name but a few. And where a book is usually by one author who lived at one time in history and had a particular point of view, a library comprises a number of authors who lived at various times in history and had many points of view.

"But wait," many Christians might object. "The Bible does have only one author and that author is God." It is true that Christians claim that God is the author of the Bible. We will discuss just what that means later when we explore the Catholic Christian understanding of the Bible as a means of handing on revelation and when we say that the authors are inspired. Nevertheless, Christians regard human beings as God's instruments in writing the Bible. These human beings lived in different centuries and had a variety of points of view.

It is extremely important to understand that the Bible is a library of books written in different literary forms, at various times in history, from a variety of points of view, because this information affects how we understand what the Bible teaches. You will find in-depth discussion of each of those topics in other articles

1

in this guide ("Understanding Genres and Literary Forms," "Understanding the Bible in Its Historical and Cultural Contexts," and "Understanding the Bible within the Living Tradition of the Catholic Church"). Here we will address another question: "How did the Bible reach its present form?"

A Five-step Process

The Bible is in finished form; that is, the library of books considered canonical is complete. But how was this particular arrangement of books decided? The Bible as we know it is the end result of what might be described as a five-step process.

Events

Though Christian faiths differ in how they read and understand the Bible, the sequence leading to the selection of particular writings to comprise the biblical canon is a five-step process. The first step is what Catholic Christians believe is God's self-revelation through events. These events occurred over a two-thousand-year period, starting with the ancestors in faith of the Jewish and Christian traditions, Abraham and Sarah, who lived around 1850 BCE, and concluding with the end of the apostolic age, that is, around the end of the first century CE. Many of the events may be familiar: Abraham responding to God's call to leave the home of his ancestors and go to a new land; Moses leading God's people out of slavery in Egypt; David uniting the twelve Tribes and establishing a united kingdom; the division of the kingdom; the rise of the Assyrians, who conquered the northern kingdom; the rise of the Babylonians, who conquered the southern kingdom and sent the people into Exile; the rise of the Persians, who

conquered the Babylonians and allowed the Israelites to return to their holy land; the rise of the Greeks and then the Romans, who ruled the holy land as part of the Roman Empire. All these events form the skeleton of the Old Testament.

It was during the time of the Roman occupation that Jesus, whom Christians believe is both human and divine, was born. The events that underlie the Gospels are: Jesus had a public ministry that was powerful in both word and deed; Jesus was found guilty of blasphemy in a Jewish court, and accused of sedition in a Roman court; Jesus received the death penalty; Jesus was crucified, died, and was buried; Jesus rose from the dead and is still in the midst of his people. The events that underlie the rest of what we call the New Testament involve the birth of the Church and the spreading of the Good News of Jesus Christ to the surrounding countries.

Oral Tradition

The second step in the process is oral tradition. People talked about the events that they experienced. Through the generations the stories of God's powerful intervention in the lives of God's people were told over and over. For example, in the Book of Genesis, the first book of the Bible, we read the stories of Abraham, Isaac, Jacob, and Joseph. As that book ends, the Israelites have gone to Egypt because there was a drought in the holy land and they needed to find food. The second book in the Bible is the Book of Exodus, in which we read the story of Moses leading the people out of slavery in Egypt. Between the last page of Genesis and the first page of Exodus, five hundred years have elapsed. The Israelites who were slaves in Egypt knew about God's promises to their ancestors not because they had a modern Bible, but because the stories of the ancestors and God's promises to the ancestors were passed on through oral tradition.

Not just stories about the events of the Old Testament were passed on through oral tradition; stories about Jesus were also passed on through oral tradition before they were written. This means that no biblical account, whether in the Old Testament or in the New Testament, is contemporary with the events that it describes. All the stories are told in hindsight. In addition, none of the stories were passed on for the purpose of teaching history. Rather, the stories are stories of faith; their purpose is to describe how God has revealed God's self through events.

The stories that developed to pass on the people's understanding of God's powerful presence in the events of their lives could be in any literary form. After all, the stories were composed not to teach history but to inspire each succeeding generation, to teach that generation that the promises made to Abraham are promises made to them, and that because they are in a covenant relationship with God, they have certain obligations and responsibilities. Such lessons could be taught in any number of forms, including legends, songs, fiction, allegories, parables, and riddles. Any literary form could be a vehicle to teach truth.

Written Tradition

Slowly, over time, some of the stories passed on through oral tradition began to be written down. If we had lived during the time of Abraham

(1850 BCE) or Moses (1250 BCE), we would not have been able to read any part of our present-day Bible. However, if we had lived during the time of King David (1000 BCE), we could have read some of what became today's Old Testament. At that time stories that had developed orally over hundreds of years were gradually written down and collected into an organized narrative.

This same process underlies the New Testament. Had we been contemporaries of Jesus, we could not have read what would become today's New Testament. Had we lived during Paul's lifetime, we could not have read the present-day Gospels, although we could have read Paul's letters, the earliest New Testament material to reach written form. Gospel materials, too, were passed on orally, and then in written form, before they became the organized narratives that we have today.

Edited Tradition

Had we lived at the time of King David and read the organized narrative that dates to about 1000 BCE, we would still not be reading the Book of Genesis or the Book of Exodus as those books now exist. Over time, in the light of subsequent events, the stories were retold to include new insights or emphasize certain points that were learned through the subsequent events. For instance, in the earliest collected narrative that dates to the time of King David, the stories of the ancestors were told from the point of view of those who lived in the south. When the kingdom split into north and south, the stories were retold from the point of view of those in the northern kingdom. After the northern kingdom was conquered by the Assyrians, those in the south pondered what the northern kingdom had done wrong. The stories were retold, emphasizing the lessons stressed by the reformers who were calling the people to fidelity to their covenant relationship with God. After the Babylonian Exile, the stories were again retold in the light of what had been learned from that experience. The Old Testament stories as they exist today are layered. They reflect the thinking and insights of the Israelites over the span of their history, not just the insights that are contemporary with the original storytellers.

The New Testament is also an edited text. The author of the Gospel According to Luke describes himself as an editor who is arranging the inherited oral and written traditions about events in order to meet the needs of his particular audience (Lk 1:1–4). Also, the order of the books in the New Testament is not the order in which the books were written. In the modern edited arrangement, the Gospels come first, and the letters, many of which were written earlier than the Gospels, follow.

Canonical

Not every book that developed through the process we have described is in the Bible. We call those books that are in the Bible, canonical. The word canon originally referred to a reed that was used to measure things, a ruler. The fact that a book is in the canon means that the believing community claims that this book is inspired by God and therefore faithfully teaches those truths that God wishes to teach for the sake of salvation. The book is a rule for faith.

The selection of canonical books also developed slowly over time.

The Old Testament canon, as it exists today, is divided into three sections by Jewish scholars: the Law, the Prophets, and the Writings. We see evidence of these divisions in the foreword to the Book of Sirach, which dates to the end of the second century BCE: "Many important truths have been handed down to us though the law, the prophets, and the later authors." However, the Hebrew canon of the Jews, which Christians call the Old Testament, probably did not reach its present form until the first century CE.

The Catholic Old Testament canon includes some books not included in the Jewish Hebrew canon or in the Protestant canon. These books—Tobit, Judith, First and Second Maccabees, Wisdom, Sirach, and Baruch—are called deuterocanonical books by Catholics and apocryphal books (that is, not part of the canon) by Protestants. All the disputed books were written during the last few hundred years before Christ, many of them in Greek. They became part of the Septuagint, that is, the Greek translation of the Hebrew Scriptures. The Hebrew Scriptures were translated into Greek in the third century BCE because many Jews lived in Egypt and spoke Greek rather than Hebrew. The deuterocanonical books appear in the Catholic canon because Catholic biblical translations rested on both the Hebrew and Greek Old Testament texts. They do not appear in Protestant canons because Protestant translations rested only on the Hebrew Old Testament texts.

Catholics and Protestants have exactly the same New Testament canon. Again, not all the books about New Testament events are in the canon. There are deuterocanonical or apocryphal gospels as well. However, by the end of the second century CE, the four Gospels that we now have were in general use, and the others had fallen out of use. By the end of the fourth century, the whole New Testament canon as we now have it had taken shape.

Christians believe that the formation of the canon was due to the work of the Holy Spirit in the worshiping community. Those books that the community recognized as faithfully passing on the beliefs of the community and nourishing the community remained in use; those that did not fell out of use.

The Catholic canon was officially closed in the sixteenth century at the Council of Trent. During the Protestant Reformation, debate arose about whether or not all the books that were then in use should be considered canonical. In reaction to this discussion, the Council affirmed that the New Testament books that had been in use for fifteen hundred years and that had formed the self-understanding of the Catholic Church were canonical. The Church would not add to them nor subtract from them.

Inspiration

Catholics affirm that God is the author of the Bible. However, Catholics do not claim that God actually wrote the Bible. The Catholic understanding is that the Bible is the end result of a process that included events, oral tradition, written tradition, editing, and acceptance by the Spirit-filled community.

Catholic belief, then, is that God is the author of the Bible in that God inspired God's people at every step of the process. Those who originally experienced the events, and recognized them as events in which God was powerful and present, were inspired. Those who passed on the stories through oral tradition, those who originally wrote them down, those who edited them, and the community that recognized certain texts as texts that accurately passed on the faith of the community were all inspired. God's inspiration was present in every generation. At the same time, the human authors of the Bible are real authors. They wrote in their own language, using their own literary expressions, and from their own historical perspectives to record the revealed word of God. Thus, the Bible is the word of God in the words of its human authors.

Revelation

What does the Church mean when it claims that the Bible is revelation? Does it mean that inspired authors had God's point of view so that every word they spoke on every subject is true (that is, literally God's word or the words that came directly from God's mouth)? No, the Church does not make such a claim, even though it affirms that the Bible is inerrant, that is, without error. When it claims that the Bible contains revelation and is inerrant, it is claiming that the Bible teaches the truth on the subjects that it is addressing: the inspired authors teach the truth about who God is, who humanity is in relation to God and the rest of creation, and what God would have people do to cooperate with the coming of God's Kingdom.

The Bible was written, then, not to teach history or science, but rather to teach about the nature of God, about how God has revealed God's self through the centuries, and about how people might live in a way that is pleasing to God. The Bible was written to teach what is necessary regarding salvation.

The Authority of the Scriptures

The Second Vatican Council's document *Dogmatic Constitution on Divine Revelation* (Dei Verbum) says, "the Christian religion itself, all the preaching of the Church must be nourished and regulated by Sacred Scripture" (no. 21). Because Christians believe that the Scriptures are God's self-revelation and that they teach the truth regarding salvation, they also believe that there is no higher authority on earth than the Scriptures. The Catholic Church teaches that the teaching Church, the Scriptures, and Tradition have a relationship in which each is essential to the other. It is the Church's role to interpret the Scriptures, but in doing so the "teaching office [Magisterium] is not above the word of God, but serves it" (*Dei Verbum,* no. 10).

This means that the Church cannot teach something that contradicts the Scriptures. However, the Church can teach a truth that has its roots, but not its full flowering, in the Scriptures, as well as something on which the Scriptures remain silent.

A Contextualist Approach to the Scriptures

Because the Catholic Church sees its role as interpreting the Scriptures, it also teaches how to understand the truth that the Bible contains. In a single word, the Church teaches its people to be contextualists, rather than fundamentalists, in interpreting the Bible. This means that in order to understand correctly the revelation that

the Bible is teaching, the reader must interpret biblical passages in the context in which they appear in the Bible. There are three contexts to consider.

Because the Bible is a library of books, the reader must consider the kind of writing, that is, the literary form, in which a particular passage appears. To ignore the literary form may cause the reader to misunderstand not only what an author is teaching on a topic but the very topic that the author is addressing.

Because the authors lived at various times in history, the reader must consider the context of each author's historical time and the presumptions that the author and the audience shared. If an author pictures God creating a flat world, the author is not teaching about the shape of the earth, but merely presuming that the earth is flat in the course of teaching that God created all that exists.

Because the Bible took form over a two-thousand-year period, the reader must consider the context of the process of revelation that occurred over time. Early insights often represent one step in understanding a mystery, not the fullness of revelation. If the reader takes a partial truth and presents it as the whole truth, he or she has once more put the authority of the Scriptures behind his or her own misunderstanding, not behind what the Bible actually teaches.

A Living Word

To be a biblical contextualist does not contradict an understanding of the Scriptures as a living word that can speak directly to the human heart in any context, any human experience. However, biblical contextualists are aware that scriptural passages taken out of context can be used to support conclusions that directly contradict the revelation that the Scriptures teach. Therefore, when a biblical contextualist hears the Scriptures as a living word, that person asks, "Is the conclusion I am drawing from this passage compatible with what the Scriptures teach as a whole?" In this way, the Christian believer feels assured of using the Scriptures to hear God's voice and not to self delude. Integrating the Scriptures into one's prayer life in this way, the Christian believes, allows the living word to help one discern God's self-revelation in one's own life, so that the Scriptures truly will be a lamp for one's feet, a light upon one's path.

Margaret Nutting Ralph, PhD
Director of the
Master of Arts Program
for Roman Catholics
Lexington Theological Seminary
Lexington, Kentucky

Understanding Genres and Literary Forms

As mentioned previously, the Bible is composed of many individual books—a library of books. The types of books in the Bible vary one from the other. The writing style of each book is different and there can even be a variety of literary forms within one book. Therefore, understanding the type of literature you are reading is essential to grasping the author's intention. Christians believe that all the books of the Bible have something to say today about God's relationship with people. Understanding the genres, literary forms, and literary techniques used by the biblical authors will be helpful for interpreting the deeper meaning of the Scriptures.

The concept of genre and literary form is not new. Bookstores organize books according to their genres. In general, the term genre is used to describe categories of literature, art, or music. The first step in correctly interpreting literature is to know its genre. For example, fiction (invented narrative) must be read and understood differently than a computer manual (technical writing) or an autobiography (a written account of one's own life). Literary forms are categories of smaller units of text that can be used within a particular genre. For example, the newspaper genre contains many literary forms, including national news stories, editorials, obituaries, sports stories, and classified ads. Even if you do it unconsciously, you must recognize the literary form of the newspaper item that you are reading in order to understand it properly. This is also true of the bibli-

cal text, which contains many different genres and literary forms such as prose, poetry, myth, law codes, historical narrative, didactic (teaching) narrative, parable, and miracle stories. It is valuable to examine the major genres and literary forms that are used in the Bible.

Genres and Literary Forms in the Old Testament

Sacred Myths, Etiologies, and Legends

Most people have only one definition for myth, assuming that it is a story once thought to be true but now proven to be false, as in the example of the ancient belief that the earth was flat. Defining myth this way would then imply that this type of literature would never appear in a book such as the Bible, believed by Christians to contain the truth revealed by God.

However, myth can be understood in more than one way. One of the most helpful definitions is provided by Margaret Nutting Ralph: "A myth is an imaginative story that uses symbols to speak about reality, but a reality that is beyond a person's comprehension. Societies compose myths to orient themselves in a moral and spiritual world" (*And God Said What?*, p. 29). In the opening eleven chapters of Genesis (also called the primeval history), the authors employ this notion of myth for understanding Creation—not how it happened but why and for what purpose. The authors use symbols and images that are

8

comprehensible to their own people in their own time to explore a truth that is beyond human comprehension. There are actually two Creation accounts in the Book of Genesis. The first appears in Genesis 1:1—2:4; the second is Genesis 2:4–25. These two stories are very different and yet the meaning and message are the same. Both of these Creation myths are intended to convey a sacred truth, namely, that God is the source of all Creation, that all Creation was made good and beautiful, that human beings are created in the "image and likeness" of God, and that God commanded humanity to be good stewards of God's Creation.

> **Many of the legends that are found in the Hebrew Bible are based on oral traditions and, for the most part, they could be described as folktales.**

Etiology is a literary form that is employed regularly in Genesis. In their book *The Old Testament,* Stephen Harris and Robert Platzner define etiologies as narratives that are intended to explain the origin or cause of some social custom, natural phenomenon, or religious ritual. However, etiologies should never be understood as historical or scientific facts but as narratives that explain the meaning or significance of something. For example, the tower of Babel story (Gn 11:1–9) explains the origin of languages, not historically, but symbolically. In the beginning, the biblical author writes, all peoples spoke the same language, but when they built the tower of Babel in an attempt to go up to God's dwelling place, God confused their languages so they would never again be able to work together to do such a thing. Thus, this story of the origin of languages is intended to teach a profound truth: God is God

and humans are not. Likewise, God's resting on the seventh day of Creation (Gn 2:2) is intended to emphasize the significance of the Sabbath as a day of rest.

Etiologies are also used to explain the origin of names and places. For example, Genesis 19:30–38 recounts the narrative of Lot and his daughters. The daughters ply their father with wine so that they can lie with him. The daughters both conceive and give birth to sons, Moab and Ammon. Conceived by deception, these boys are the progenitors of the Moabites and the Ammonites who become the rivals of Israel. There are many other examples of etiologies found in the Old Testament.

Another narrative form that appears with frequency in the Hebrew Bible is legend. Legends are based in history. However, legends are different from history insofar as history involves the retelling of past events about which there is a written record or the details can otherwise be documented as factual, whereas legend does not. Many of the legends that are found in the Hebrew Bible are based on oral traditions and, for the most part, they could be described as folktales. These stories were passed on orally through many generations, so the telling and retelling also affect the nature of the stories. Legends are characterized by exaggeration, the use of magical details, etiologies, and the folk customs of the storytellers. Thus, legends are not necessarily factual. However, they were preserved because they convey important truths. In the case of the Hebrew Bible, legends are frequently a means for God's revelation.

The stories of Israel's ancient ancestors recounted in Genesis chapters 12 through 50 have all the characteristics of legends. They contain the stories of betrothal and hospitality, of the naming of sacred places, and they recall the origin of family tribes. More important, God is revealed in these stories. The relationship of God and God's people is established through a sacred Covenant, which is renewed with each of the great patriarchs and matriarchs—Abraham and Sarah, Isaac and Rebecca, and Jacob and his wives and sons. These wonderful stories speak to us of God and set the stage for what is to follow in the Scriptures.

Hebrew Poetry

Examples of Hebrew poetry abound in the Old Testament. Scholars suggest up to one-third of the Hebrew Bible is written in poetic form, and some of the most beautiful examples are in the Book of Psalms. The Psalter (Book of Psalms) contains one hundred and fifty individual psalms composed over a span of approximately six centuries. They reflect the prayerful expressions of their authors—at times ecstatic praise and at other times the depths of despair. Scholars categorize the psalms into several types: hymns or songs of praise, psalms of thanksgiving, laments (both individual and communal), royal psalms, and wisdom psalms. Although the psalms originated as Jewish prayers, Christians today regularly use them as well in their worship services as well.

In addition to the Psalms, several other books of the Old Testament contain a great deal of poetry. They differ, however, in the fact that they do not share the same subject matter. For example, the psalms were used for temple worship, but the Song of Songs (also called the Song of Solomon) is an erotic love song about a woman searching for her beloved. Other books like Job, Proverbs, Ecclesiastes, the Wisdom of Solomon, and Sirach, often called wisdom literature, deal with universal human concerns like the problem of suffering, how good people are rewarded, how the wicked are punished, and what it means to be wise or what it takes to be successful in God's eyes.

Like the poetry of other cultures of its day, Hebrew poetry has some distinctive characteristics that are different from our own poetry. Unlike our classic understandings of modern poetry that includes certain rhythms and rhyming sounds, Hebrew poetry uses thought parallelisms. Biblical scholars have identified three commonly used thought parallelisms: synonymous, antithetical, and synthetic. Synonymous parallelism consists of a phrase or sentence followed by a phrase or sentence that has the same meaning, even in each of its parts. Here is an example:

Have pity on me, Lord, for I am weak;
>   heal me, Lord, for my bones are
>>   trembling. (Ps 6:3)

Antithetical parallelism consists of a phrase or sentence followed by a phrase or sentence that is its opposite:

The lips of the wise disseminate
>   knowledge,
>>   but the heart of fools is perverted.
>>>   (Prv 15:7)

Finally, synthetic parallelism consists of two lines, the first of which is completed by the second. Here is an example of two synthetic parallelisms, one following the other:

A shield before me is God
   who saves the honest heart.
God is a just judge,
   who rebukes in anger every day.

(Ps 7:11–12)

Prophetic Literature

There are fifteen prophetic books in the Hebrew Bible: Isaiah, Jeremiah, Ezekiel, and the twelve minor prophets. Christians include the Book of Daniel among the prophets, but in the Hebrew Bible it is included with the writings, because, for the most part, it is an apocalyptic work. In addition, several of the historical books (1 and 2 Samuel and 1 and 2 Kings) contain stories about some of the earliest prophets like Elijah and Elisha, as well as some of the forms most often associated with prophecy—the oracle and symbolic acts.

The books of the writing prophets, of which Amos is probably the earliest, are purported to contain the words of the prophet himself as he or his secretary had written them. Biblical scholars think that these oracles—brief, poetic utterances that contain a message or pronouncement from God—first circulated as collections of sayings, which were later rearranged, edited, and expanded by the addition of narrative. After decades and centuries of this kind of literary work, the writings that we now call the prophetic books came into being.

The primary purpose of prophecy, according to Christian thought, is to make known God's will for the people. Prophets serve as spokespersons for God or intermediaries between God and the people. God delivers the oracle to the prophet, sometimes in answer to a question or as a response to a request for a sign, but always on God's initiative alone. That is, the prophet does not control God's word. At times prophecies have a predictive character, but that is not their primary or exclusive purpose. Rather, their messages fall into two categories: oracles of judgment or oracles of salvation. In an oracle of judgment, the prophet brings accusation against God's people for failing to keep the Covenant. In an oracle of salvation, the prophet delivers God's message of consolation in times of trouble and God's promise to rescue them from their suffering.

Often oracles are obscure and difficult to interpret, because their meaning depends on the historical and social situation in which they were given. Oracles can be as brief as a word or sentence, or they can be quite long. They can also take the form of reported visions or dreams (Is chap. 6). They sometimes appear as songs of lament (Jer 14:1–10) or songs of love (Is chap. 40).

Some prophets used symbolic actions to reveal God's message. In the opening chapters of Ezekiel, the prophet engages in several eye-catching actions. He dramatically cuts his hair and beard, scattering some of the hair to the wind, some he throws into the fire, some is attacked by sword, and finally a remnant is sewn into the hem of his garment. The reader is told that the hair represents the fate of the people of Judah (see the introduction to Ezekiel). In a second striking display, Ezekiel is told to make a drawing of the city of Jerusalem on a clay brick, build siege walls against it, and arrange camps and battering rams around it, once again acting out the fate of Israel. Later the prophet carries all that he has in a sack as he crawls in and out of the city through a hole in the wall. Each of these actions is intended to tell the people what will happen to them if they fail to return to living faithfully the Covenant.

Other Literary Forms

The writers of Old Testament literature used a variety of literary forms to evoke a response from the reader and to express deep feelings. In addition to the ones we have already mentioned, we should add simile (comparisons using like or as), metaphor (comparisons that do not use like or as), parables (fictional narratives that involve a comparison and that contain some sort of surprising twist), allegory (objects or actions in a narrative that function as a symbol of something else), and personification (giving human attributes to an idea or abstract concept).

There are many more literary forms that appear with some regularity in the Old Testament: genealogies, narratives (fictional and didactic), sagas, and debates. Though this is not a comprehensive list, it highlights the importance of considering the literary form when interpreting a passage from the Scriptures. If you read carefully, you will recognize when the biblical author is using one or more of these literary forms and you will be able to interpret the text accordingly. Then you will see the richness of this ancient literature and appreciate how it can be read with new eyes in every generation.

Genres and Literary Forms in the New Testament

The Gospels

The New Testament also contains a variety of genres and literary forms. The Gospels According to Matthew, Mark, Luke, and John represent a unique literary genre whose origin is unknown. Although it has some superficial similarities with the biography and the history, the Gospel genre is quite different. The Gospel is historical, but the Gospel writer was not intending to write a history. Some scholars think that the gospel—the term means "good news"—was developed by the early Christian community to proclaim faith in Jesus Christ by telling the story of his life, death, and Resurrection, and how Jesus' life and ministry had affected theirs. The Gospels as they are known today evolved in stages over several decades. Beginning with oral traditions, the stories of Jesus were gathered, written down, and eventually arranged and edited into the Gospels we have today. The Gospels in their final form contain a variety of literary forms, some of which will be explored here.

Parables and Allegories

One literary form that appears frequently in the Gospels, especially in Matthew and Mark, is the parable. A parable is a fictional narrative (story) that functions like an extended simile or metaphor. Jesus' parables often begin, "the kingdom of heaven is like . . ." (e.g., Mt 13:31). Because parables are essentially riddles, the story also must include an unexpected twist of events. This surprise ending is meant to bring the listener to a moment of discovery, but sometimes it is difficult for us to appreciate the riddle because we do not understand the cultural world in which the parable was originally told. For example, in the parable of the prodigal son (Lk 15:11–32), the graciousness of the father is shocking. This is a man who apparently had wealth and great status in his community, and here he is waiting for and even running after his wayward son, who had earlier told him that he was as good as dead in his eyes because he asked for his inheritance while his father was still living. The son had shamed his father by asking for his inheritance, and then the father shamed himself by receiving back his son in such a generous way. Jesus used parables like this one as a very effective means of teaching.

On occasion parables can be interpreted as allegories. Allegories are stories with deeper levels of meaning, in which every character or event is a symbol for something else. Among the Gospel parables, the parable of the sower (Mt 13:3–9, Mk 4:3–9, Lk 8:5–8) is a good example of an allegory. After Jesus tells the parable to the disciples, the narrator of the Gospel explains it to his disciples, demonstrating its allegorical nature. The seed that is sown is the word of God. The places where the seed falls represent the hearts of believers and nonbelievers. One who has faith will see the true meaning of this story. Both parables and allegories are powerful teaching tools that Jesus uses effectively in his ministry. They invite us to deeper faith.

> **On occasion parables can be interpreted as allegories. Allegories are stories with deeper levels of meaning.**

The Letters

The New Testament contains twenty-one letters. Thirteen of them are attributed to Paul. Of those thirteen, seven are considered to be authentic letters of Paul (Pauline). The others were written anonymously, but attributed to Paul as a way of extending his memory to later generations of Christians (Deutero-Pauline). Still others are attributed to various apostles and leaders of the early Church, including Peter, James, Jude, and John. The letter genre follows a basic stylistic pattern that has four elements: the opening formula, the thanksgiving, the body of the letter, and the closing. This letter-writing format is not unique to the New Testament. Rather, it was used by Jews, Greeks, and Romans for all types of written communication.

In the opening formula of a letter, the letter writer first identifies himself and then the intended recipients, followed by a blessing. The thanksgiving section is next. In it, the letter writer comments on his relationship to the recipients as a way of establishing rapport, and he also introduces the themes of the letter. The body of the letter contains the letter writer's message. It may contain a teaching, answers to the recipients' questions, or even ethical exhortations. The conclusion of these letters contains personal greetings, travel instructions, and a blessing.

Most of the New Testament letters were intended for the entire congregation, to be read publicly when the community was gathered together.

However, one letter, the Letter to Philemon, has as its primary addressee an individual within a community. Some letters are considered to be circular letters, because the letter writer expected that they be copied and shared with other church communities.

Apocalyptic Literature

Apocalyptic (derived from the Greek word meaning "revelation") literature was rather common in the third century BCE through the second century CE. In general, this type of literature involves the revelation of secrets of the cosmos (literally, "the world"), including the workings of the heavenly bodies, the fixing of the calendar, the names and activities of angelic beings, and the places of reward and punishment. They also include secrets about the future, like political and historical events, the destiny of God's people, and so on. Sometimes the seer is allowed to journey to heavenly locations. In those cases, the apocalypse also describes the details of the heavenly journey. Most apocalypses also include a command to the seer to seal the written account of the visions for some future time.

Because of its link to the end-times, apocalyptic literature is frequently referred to as "crisis literature," because it generally appears in the context of historical, political, or religious turmoil. However, modern readers sometimes mistakenly interpret the Book of Revelation as a roadmap or itinerary of the end-times. In fact, although much of the text is written in future tense, the historical author intended it to be a critique of situations in his own day. In particular, it addresses the problem of evil in the world by asserting that God is all-powerful and just and that God will indeed reward the righteous and punish the wicked. It's just a matter of time! (For a more in-depth discussion on the literary forms of the Letters and Revelation, see the Introduction to the Letters and Revelation.)

Shannon Schrein, OSF, PhD
Professor and Chair
of Religious Studies
Lourdes College
Sylvania, Ohio

Understanding the Bible in Its Historical and Cultural Contexts

Often when someone starts reading the Bible, he or she is seeking some spiritual comfort or guidance. Many new readers simply assume that the Bible will immediately make sense and can be directly applied to their everyday concerns.

Certainly there is truth to this assumption. A person can read such passages as Psalm 23:1, "The Lord is my shepherd," or Jesus' words of comfort in Matthew 11:28, "Come to me, all you who labor and are burdened, and I will give you rest," and get immediate benefit from them. The Ten Commandments (Ex chap. 20, Dt chap. 5) can also be fairly easy to understand. But the fact is, sooner or later, the beginning reader will encounter some difficulties. The reader will come across many passages that at first glance will be puzzling, seem irrelevant, or may even be offensive. In the Old Testament, the reader will encounter long lists of unpronounceable names, graphic accounts of ancient wars and battles, stories of men marrying multiple women and having sexual relations with their slaves, and detailed instructions on offering animals as sacrifices to God. In the New Testament, the reader will meet with heated debates on whether male children should be circumcised, commandments encouraging slaves to obey their masters, a long discussion on why women must wear head coverings in church, and bizarre visions of monsters with seven heads arising from the sea. If the reader wishes to make sense out of passages such as these, help is needed.

Historical, Cultural Contexts Key to Understanding

One of the greatest helps in understanding the Bible is recognizing that it was written many years ago and from within cultures very different from our own. The biblical authors often refer to past events with which we are no longer familiar. Their overall views of the world and assumptions about how society should be set up are very different from our own. Clearly, modern readers need to become familiar with the history and cultures of the biblical writers in order to better understand the message they were trying to convey.

The historical and cultural approach to understanding biblical texts immediately raises some legitimate concerns. After all, the Christian reader may ask, isn't the Bible the word of God? And if God is eternal and unchanging, then shouldn't God's word be eternal and unchanging? If this is true, then why would modern readers need to learn about the historical and cultural contexts in which the Bible was written? God's unchanging word should apply just as directly to modern culture as it applied to the ancient cultures in which it was written. (See the chart on page 168 on the Historical Critical Method of Scripture Analysis.)

Though this line of thinking may seem logical, on closer inspection it turns out to be too simplistic. Christians of all denominations do indeed accept the Bible as the word of God, but they will also have to admit that

God did not write the Bible directly. Rather, Christian belief is that God chose to use humans to write the various books of the Bible. Christians believe that God inspired and guided these human authors, but God didn't remove all their particularly human perspectives. God respected the biblical authors' humanity, and inspired them as ordinary human beings who thought and acted in much the same manner as any other human being of their time and culture. (See article, "What Is the Bible?")

Applying the Historical Critical Method to Genesis

Let's apply our discussion to the first account of Creation in the Bible, the account of God creating the world in six days and resting on the seventh (Gn 1:1—2:4). If we simply read this Creation story without a sense of the historical and cultural context in which the story was written, our natural tendency would be to understand this as a literal account of how God created all things in six days, finishing with the creation of humans on the sixth day. If we read the rest of Genesis in the same literal manner, adding up the life spans of the various people, beginning with Adam and Eve and reaching into the times of documented history, we could conclude that the earth is less than five thousand years old.

Now this literal understanding of Genesis conflicts with the modern understanding of the earth's origins in dozens of ways. First, there is obviously a vast discrepancy in time: a literal reading of Genesis places the age of the earth at less than five thousand years, while the best scientific estimates are that the earth is about 4.5 billion years old. Science tells us that the sun was formed billions of years before the earth, yet Genesis says that God created the sun on the fourth day, after separating the seas and the dry land on earth on the third. Science and our own experience of the world tell us that plants need the sun to grow; Genesis tells us that the earth brought forth plants on the third day, one day before the sun was created. The discrepancies could easily be multiplied.

Some people see only two options at this point. One is to accept modern science and reject the Bible as false; the other is to accept Genesis as true and reject modern science as false. There is, however, a third alternative, and this involves taking the historical context of Genesis into account in our understanding.

We are not sure who wrote Genesis. A traditional answer is that Moses is the author, but Genesis itself does not make this claim. Most biblical scholars think that ancient Israelite writers recorded these stories based on the oral traditions of their communities and eventually shaped them into a coherent narrative. In the case of the Creation story, the authors of Genesis seem to have combined two originally separate stories. Most biblical scholars recognize two very different accounts of God's Creation in Genesis, one in Genesis 1:1—2:4, and the other in Genesis 2:4–25. (Compare the details in both accounts.) These two stories are in fact much closer to the traditional stories about the origin of the world told in other cultures than to a scientific account that details exactly how the earth was formed.

Now we know that the Israelite authors of Genesis did not have access to modern scientific information about the origin of the world. They probably had never seen a dinosaur fossil and they would not have had use of modern scientific methods to determine its age if they had. If God had communicated modern scientific information about the earth's creation—light-years, big bang explosions, quantum physics, and evolution—neither the Israelite authors nor their readers would have understood. And so according to Christian belief, God inspired the writers to communicate in ways that made sense in the authors' own time and culture.

An All-Powerful yet Understandable God

Most biblical scholars agree that the authors of the Book of Genesis chose these stories to communicate a message about God's relationship to the created world, about why the world was created, and about what God intended as humanity's responsibilities toward the rest of Creation (see "Understanding Genres and Literary Forms"). In contrast with their non-Israelite neighbors, who told stories about warring deities who created the world out of the spoils of battle and made humans to serve as slaves of the deities, the authors of Genesis asserted in story form that the God of Israel was all-powerful—creating only by speaking a word and declaring everything to be good. These same stories make the point that God so treasured human beings that he made them in his image and likeness, and God gave them responsibility to participate in Creation by populating the earth and being stewards of the land. Finally, these Genesis stories describe a creator God who has compassion on human beings even when they disobey him.

And what is the significance of the seven days of Creation, in which God rested on the seventh day? Many biblical scholars think that this detail of the first Creation story in Genesis reflects the fact that Israelites of the authors' time were already observing Sabbath rest. How better to make the point that God intended this practice than to say that God also rested from work on the seventh day of Creation? The author was expressing God's activity at the human level, in words and concepts with which people were familiar.

Does God's Word Change?

In the Old Testament, God commands his people to offer sacrifices of grain or animals as a way of worshiping God (see, for example, the detailed description in Leviticus, chapters 1 through 7). We may assume that the first followers of Jesus, who were all Jews, continued to follow these commandments. But within several decades after the death and Resurrection of Jesus, these commandments were no longer followed, either by Jews or by those who had come to be called Christians. For first-century Jews and Jewish Christians, the reason was obvious: the Jerusalem Temple where these sacrifices had been offered had been destroyed. Gentile (non-Jewish) Christians, on the other hand, had never offered sacrifices in the Temple in the first place. Thus, early Christians needed to explain why God's word commanded the offering of sacrifices, when they in fact were not offering them. One early Christian answer, found in the Letter to the Hebrews, is that Jesus' death on the cross was the ultimate sacrifice that removed the need to offer further sacrifices as a means of worshiping God.

From a human point of view, it might appear that God's word had changed. At one point in history, working with a certain people (the ancient Israelites) in a certain culture, God required sacrifices of grain and animals (see the introduction to Leviticus). At a later point in history, however, these sacrifices were no longer required. Clearly, then, the laws of sacrifice applied only to a certain time and culture. Even if, from a Christian perspective, we say that God used the old sacrifices as a preparation for, or foreshadowing of, the ultimate sacrifice of Christ, we still must acknowledge that certain aspects of the Bible can only be understood as applying to or being relevant for their ancient historical and cultural contexts.

Notice, however, that it is too simplistic, even wrong, to conclude that the Old Testament only applied to the ancient Israelite culture and is no longer relevant for Christians today. According to Roman Catholic teaching, "both the Old and the New Testaments in their entirety, with all their parts, are sacred and canonical" (*Dei Verbum,* no. 11). Christians still follow the Ten Commandments and the commandment to "love your neighbor as yourself" (Lv 19:18). They are called to obey the teachings of the prophets on the need to care for the poor and oppressed (Martin Luther King Jr., for example, quoted from the prophet Amos [5:24] in his famous "I have a dream" speech). Roman Catholic teaching would have the reader, with the guidance of the Church, discern between what is limited to a certain time and culture and what transcends those cultural limitations and still applies today.

The New Testament and Slavery

For Christians, it is perhaps not too surprising that some aspects of the Old Testament would apply only to ancient times and cultures. The stories seem strange to many, and some of their many images of God difficult to comprehend. But are there also examples where certain aspects of the New Testament are similarly limited in their relevance for today?

Let's take the example of slavery. Christianity began and spread in the Roman Empire, an empire whose economy was based on slave labor. The New Testament authors simply accept the institution of slavery as a normal part of life. They never call for an end to slavery. They do admonish masters to treat their slaves well (Eph 6:9, Col 4:1; see also Paul's Letter to Philemon, where Paul is sending a runaway slave back to his master, encouraging the master to treat the slave as a "brother"). Slaves, in turn, are to "be obedient to your human masters with fear and trembling, in sincerity of heart, as to Christ" (Eph 6:5; see also Col 3:22, 1 Tm 6:1, Ti 2:9–10, 1 Pt 2:18).

Now it is a historical fact that the Southern slave owners in the United States before the Civil War used the Bible to justify slavery. Neither the Old nor the New Testament, they rightly pointed out, ever condemned slavery. So they concluded that if the Bible is the eternal word of God, its teaching must still apply.

No Christian today defends slavery. The Church, as well as modern society, has come to see that it is inherently evil for one person to own another person, no matter how well the master treats his or her slave. We see this development in Pope Gregory XVI's prohibition of Christians from engaging in slavery or the slave trade (In *Supremo Apostolatus,* 1839). Though acknowledging that the Bible itself permitted slavery, Gregory traced a movement in papal teaching toward an ever clearer awareness of the dignity and rights of every human, culminating in his own prohibition. Society in the ancient world had not yet reached this level of moral insight, and so naturally, the biblical authors reflect that stage of moral development.

The Great Paradox within Christian Belief

At the center of Christian faith is the belief that the Son of God chose to enter the world in human form in the person of Jesus. The divine Son of God "emptied himself, / taking the form of a slave, / . . . he humbled himself, / becoming obedient to death, / even death on a cross" (Phil 2:7–8). All this he did in order to reach out to humans in their limitations and weakness.

The Catholic Church teaches that God chose to speak in a similar way through the Bible. God's eternal, unchanging word has "taken on flesh" in the human words of the Bible (see *Dei Verbum,* no. 13). God chose to express his word through humans, who act and write as human authors, with all their limitations and weaknesses. Therefore, to understand and interpret better God's revealed word, the reader of the Bible must inquire about the historical and cultural contexts of its human authors. This is the great paradox within Christian belief—that God entrusted his eternal word to humanity in the Bible, but it comes through limited human authors. This paradox calls for discernment, the Church teaches. The reader, guided by the wisdom of Church teaching, must be able to distinguish between the eternal truth and the limited cultural expression of that truth. The Christian cannot avoid this discernment process, because the word of God comes to us only through human means.

Martin Albl, PhD
Associate Professor
of Religious Studies
Presentation College
Aberdeen, South Dakota

Understanding the Bible within the Living Tradition of the Catholic Church

Even though the Bible tops the all-time list of bestsellers, it is a complicated, richly textured collection of texts compiled over nearly two thousand years. Unlike most books, it does not have a clear story line, so reading it from start to finish does not yield clear comprehension. It contains repetitions (such as the two accounts of Creation in the initial chapters of Genesis), strange customs, tongue-twisting names, and some disturbing passages.

Moreover, the vast majority of us read the Bible in translation, because it was originally written in Hebrew and Greek, with some occasional Aramaic. In fact, as of 2004, translations of the complete Bible were available in 422 languages. The New Testament alone is available in 1,079 languages. Overall, some portions of the Bible are available in 2,377 different languages—testimony to the importance of the Scriptures throughout the world.

Catholics belong to a Tradition that reverences the Scriptures as sacred, mediating God's revealing word. As hallowed literature, the Bible is central to Catholic, Christian identity; it is a means by which Catholics deepen their relationship with the divine and learn how to live covenantal love. Catholics are taught that they have a responsibility to ponder its texts with heart, soul, and mind, and to engage in the holy work of seeking to understand in order to live in accord with its revelation.

This holy work of seeking understanding is called biblical interpretation. Every text, of course, must be interpreted: words are layered with meaning and have many implications. Because the words of the Scriptures originated in another world—antiquity—the reader must seek to enter into this realm with its sensibilities and assumptions that are far different from modern ones. The intricate process by which the Bible was formed requires that the reader patiently draw out meanings rather than presuppose that an initial reading is what the text means.

Interpretation, especially in the Catholic Tradition, is a communal responsibility rather than an individual's exclusive right. Over the ages, the Catholic Church has acquired a rich treasury of biblical interpretation in varied forms: sermons, scholarly discourse, liturgical texts, stained-glass windows, paintings, sculptures, drama, architecture, and music. On certain occasions, church councils or commissions have issued statements formalizing the ways that the Scriptures should be understood. The Council of Trent (between 1545 and 1563), for instance, forbade private interpretation, decreeing that "no one, relying on his own prudence, twist Holy Scripture in matters of faith and morals that pertain to the edifice of Christian doctrine, according to his own mind" (*The Christian Faith in the Doctrinal Documents of the Catholic Church*, no. 1507). Many apparently thought Trent was forbidding personal reading of the Scriptures; an unintended consequence of this decree was that generations of Catholics grew up unfamiliar with the Bible. The Second Vatican Council (1962–1965), however, gave new life to biblical study: "Easy access to Sacred Scripture should be provided for all the Christian faithful" (*Dei Verbum,* no. 22).

Thanks to Vatican Council II, biblical study came of age in Catholicism after the 1960s. People flocked to Bible studies and courses, new books flooded the market, and a nearly fifteen-hundred-page analysis by Catholic scholars, The Jerome Biblical Commentary, appeared in 1968 (with a revised edition in 1990). Amid this flowering of interest and knowledge, the Pontifical Biblical Commission (PBC), a body of some twenty biblical scholars from all over the world, issued several documents that synthesize Catholic principles of interpretation. Three are of particular importance: *The Historical Truth of the Gospels* (1964), *The Interpretation of the Bible in the Church* (1993), and *The Jewish People and Their Sacred Scriptures in the Christian Bible* (2002). From time to time, other Church agencies issue statements that contribute to the distinctive character of a Catholic reading of the Bible.

The Catholic Church and Interpreting the Scriptures

At the core of Catholic thinking is the principle that the Bible is the "word of God in human language" (*The Interpretation of the Bible in the Church* [*IBC*], I.A.a). Just as the Scriptures mediate the divine-human encounter, it is simultaneously divine and human: ". . . the whole Bible comes at once from God and from the inspired human author" (*IBC*, III.D.2.c).

In reading the Bible, Catholics seek knowledge of God's ways in the belief that God communicates with humanity. Catholic readers ponder the texts not simply for their meanings but for the knowledge the text cultivates in them—to be the kind of people God desires.

But the Church teaches that we discern God's voice only through the medium of human language. God speaks in the images, customs, and idioms of particular people in specific cultures, not in some timeless, abstract mode. Vatican Council II makes an analogy to the Incarnation: just as Christ took on human nature, so, too, did God "take on" human language in the revelatory process (*Dei Verbum,* no. 13). Acknowledging that the human authors of the Scriptures were true authors allows the reader to admit that the authors whom God inspired were, nevertheless, finite and scarred, as we all are, by cultural biases and ignorance. Thus, the reader finds troubling passages, such as Jephthah's sacrifice of his daughter in order to fulfill a vow (Jgs 11), or images of a violent, vengeful God, such as God's order to Saul to slay the Amalekites (1 Sm 15), or the assertion that "it is improper for a woman to speak in the church" (1 Cor 14:35). If the reader takes biblical texts at face value, he or she is apt to misunderstand their meaning; texts must be situated in their time and place: "Certain biblical narratives present aspects of disloyalty or cruelty which today would be morally inadmissible, but they must be understood in their historical and literary contexts" (*The Jewish People and Their Sacred Scrip-*

tures in the Christian Bible, no. 87).

Learning the art of interpretation is all the more imperative for the reader who finds in biblical texts real consequences for how to live. As the article "Understanding the Bible in Its Historical and Cultural Contexts" points out, it took far too long for many Christian interpreters to grasp the incompatibility of slavery with the overall biblical message. Yet, how biblical texts on slavery were construed offers vivid testimony to the importance of the interpretative process. Although slavery is no longer a hotly debated topic, how we read biblical texts today about the role of women, capital punishment, homosexuality, relations between Jews and Christians, and care for the earth remains very much at issue. For Catholics, drawing upon the Bible in addressing contemporary issues demands diligence, patience, and an understanding of how Tradition functions in the Church.

One of the most tragic examples of misinterpretation is how Christians, including Catholics, have failed to situate anti-Jewish texts in their historical and literary contexts. Those who read the New Testament may note how many texts depict Jews in negative ways. Matthew 23:1–36 may be the most extensive portrayal of the Pharisees as hypocrites and legalists—and thus as foils for the teaching of Jesus—but it is only one among many. Generations of preachers and teachers have read the prophets as if their messianic images provided such a clear and compelling portrait that every Jew should have recognized Jesus as the Messiah. Not knowing the

context of Paul's letters, many have oversimplified his complex teaching about the Law by contrasting the freedom of the followers of Christ with the oppressive obligations the Law imposes on Jews. For nearly two thousand years, the Church held "the Jews" responsible for the death of Jesus.

Jews have paid a terrible cost for such interpretations. Blaming Jews for the death of Jesus meant that for centuries Christians taunted them as "Christ-killers." Such derisive speech often led to violence against Jews: burning of synagogues and sacred texts, expulsions from various countries, confinement in ghettoes, torture, and death. It symbolized what French historian Jules Isaac has called the "teaching of contempt"—the long legacy of Christian teaching and preaching that disparaged Jews and Judaism. In the words of the Catholic bishops of France, an "anti-Jewish tradition" marked Christian doctrine, teaching, preaching, and liturgy for centuries. It provided the ground for the flourishing of "the venomous plant of hatred for the Jews" (*Catholics Remember the Holocaust*, p. 34). Centuries of anti-Jewish teaching and preaching were key factors in Christian complicity in the Shoah (Holocaust).

When Christians misinterpreted the Bible, they did this at great cost. By using their sacred texts against Jews, Christians betrayed the very Gospel they proclaimed. By reading their Scriptures out of context, Christians distorted their relationships with Jews and oversimplified their own story. They missed much of the

> **By using their sacred texts against Jews, Christians betrayed the very Gospel they proclaimed.**

prophetic power of the ministry of Jesus, the rich diversity of the early church, and its complicated process of forming an identity apart from Judaism. They missed the way in which church and synagogue are siblings.

Only in the past fifty years have the churches begun to confront the tragic consequences of their teaching of contempt—thanks in many respects to a meeting that Jules Isaac had with Pope John XXIII in 1960 that ultimately resulted in the Catholic Church's relationship with the Jewish people being put on the agenda of the Second Vatican Council (1962–1965). The decree of that Council, *Nostra Aetate (Declaration on the Relation of the Church to Non-Christian Religions)*, inaugurated a revolution in Christian understandings of Judaism. Many subsequent Church documents have developed a dramatic new framework for thinking about Christianity in relation to Judaism.

Although the section about the relationship between the Catholic Church and Judaism in *Nostra Aetate* is brief, it is revolutionary. In saying that Christ's "passion cannot be charged against all the Jews, without distinction, then alive, nor against the Jews of today," the Council turned in a new direction toward the Jewish people. Rather than blaming and condemning the Jewish people for the death of Jesus, as had been the case for much of Church history, the Council declared that "the Jews should not be presented as rejected or accursed by God, as if this followed from the Holy Scriptures" (no. 4).

In the years since Vatican Council II, Catholic thinking has expanded and developed what *Nostra Aetate* initiated. Now a body of documentation helps Catholics interpret passages that seem to make Jews alone responsible for Jesus' death or portray the Pharisees as legalistic hypocrites. In 1988 the United States Conference of Catholic Bishops (USCCB) published *God's Mercy Endures Forever: Guidelines on the Presentation of Jews and Judaism in Catholic Preaching.* These guidelines explain how, once the Church had separated from and distanced itself from Judaism, the Church tended to "telescope" the process by which the Gospels were composed late in the first century CE. The guidelines explain how some of the controversies in the Gospels between Jesus and the Pharisees may actually have taken place between church leaders and rabbis toward the end of the first century and "were 'read back' into the life of Jesus" (no. 20). This principle helps reorient understanding of the Pharisees: "Jesus was perhaps closer to the Pharisees in his religious vision than to any other group of his time" (*God's Mercy Endures Forever,* no. 19).

An essential concept in contemporary Catholic approaches to the Bible is that sound understanding of the New Testament depends in large measure on knowledge of Judaism in the Second Temple Period, ca. 540 BCE to 70 CE. For example, knowing about the varied ways Judaism was understood and practiced during this period helps one place Jesus and those who followed him within these "Judaisms." The disastrous consequences of the Jewish War against the Romans (66–70) contributed to the intensity of the family arguments that developed during the period of the formation of the Gospels over whether the Way of Torah or the Way of Jesus was the primary path to God. The negative depictions of

Jews in the Gospels reflect this post-70 CE period and largely manifest a family argument that was no longer understood once the Church was composed almost exclusively of Gentiles (non-Jews). Thus, in reading the New Testament, it is imperative to recognize that the "human language" is colored by polemic and to look for guidance from the Church so that anti-Jewish misinterpretations will no longer be a part of Christianity. The developments in Catholic biblical teaching since *Nostra Aetate* witness to the holy works of seeking understanding of the Sacred Scriptures and doing justice to the Church's relationship with Judaism.

Conclusion

According to Catholic Church teaching, if we are to hear God's revelation in texts from antiquity, then we must respect the context in which it is expressed. This requires self-discipline, lest we impose assumptions from our world on texts that originated in a very different world. Prooftexting, in which a verse is wrenched from its context to make a point, fails to respect the way in which God's word is expressed in human language; it ignores the particularity in which and by which God reveals.

The affirmation that the Bible is God's word in human language provides a critical principle for interpretation: Situate the Scriptures in the world from which they came before exploring what they mean for our world. Placing texts in context typically involves drawing upon some of the resources available from those steeped in knowledge of the history, culture, and literary provenance of the Bible. In part, this involves using the findings of those who employ a method known as historical criticism—methodologies that offer ways of illuminating the world out of which ancient texts come. It includes careful attention to language, to the cultural and historical contexts, and to the various ways in which texts were edited as they became part of a larger unit. Historical criticism is an important tool for Catholic biblical interpreters, in fact, it is "indispensable" (*IBC*, I.A.). (See previous articles on "Understanding Genres and Literary Forms," "Understanding the Bible in Its Historical and Cultural Contexts," and the chart on Historical Criticism.) But historical criticism never exhausts the meaning of a text. As a classic, the Bible's meanings transcend what they meant in the past; it is essential to look to how the believing community today grapples with them. As knowledge increases and new insights and perspectives develop, the Catholic Church sees biblical texts in a new light.

In contrast, fundamentalism, according to the PBC, "refuses to admit that the inspired word of God has been expressed in human language and that this word has been expressed, under divine inspiration, by human authors possessed of limited capacities and resources" (*IBC*, I.F). Fundamentalism tends to regard biblical texts as word-for-word dictation, which may be attractive to those who look to the Bible for ready answers to life's problems, but it ultimately offers a "false certitude." A fundamentalist interpretation, the Catholic Church teaches, "unwittingly confuses the divine substance of the biblical message with what are in fact its human limitations" (*IBC*, I.F).

The Catholic Church's insistence that the Sacred Scriptures are the "word of God [expressed] in human language" (*IBC,* I.A.a.) frees readers from anxiety about the inconsistencies and even idiosyncrasies of biblical texts, and allows them to appreciate the diverse, creative ways human authors communicated their experience and understanding of God's saving presence.

Mary C. Boys, SNJM, PhD
Skinner and McAlpin
Professor of Practical Theology
Union Theological Seminary
New York

English Translations of the Bible

The Bible was not originally written in English. The books of the Old Testament were first written in Hebrew, with some passages (parts of Ezra and Daniel) written in Aramaic, a language closely related to Hebrew. The books of the New Testament were first written in Greek.

This article explores the process of how one translates from these ancient languages into English, provides an overview of the history of English translations, and considers some of the issues of interpretation that are raised in the translation process.

Textual Criticism: Getting Back to the Original Text

Many people realize, correctly, that the books of the Bible were written centuries ago, but then incorrectly assume that translations of the Bible have also been passed down for that same length of time. The reality is that modern Bible versions are based not on older translations but rather on ancient copies of the original books themselves.

To illustrate how the Bible is translated, let's take a particular book—the Gospel of Luke—as an example. Luke wrote in Greek, somewhere around the years 80–90 CE. He most likely wrote with ink on papyrus, a writing material not too different from our modern paper. Now the problem for readers today is that the actual Gospel that Luke wrote is lost. In fact, we no longer have the original manuscript of any book of the Bible. So this raises an obvious concern: How do we know what the biblical

authors wrote if we no longer have their original writings?

Fortunately, we do have ancient copies of these biblical books, known as manuscripts (the word manuscript literally means "written by hand"). In the case of the New Testament writings, we have more than 5,300 Greek manuscripts of various parts of the New Testament, together with thousands of other early translations or quotations of the New Testament books by other ancient authors. The earliest manuscript evidence is a fragment of the Gospel of John, dated to around the year 125 CE (that is, only about 25 years after the Gospel was written). In the case of the Old Testament writings, the discovery of the Dead Sea scrolls has allowed scholars access to numerous copies, many dating well before the time of Jesus, of virtually every book of the Old Testament.

Let's return now to our example. In an effort to recover as nearly as possible what Luke wrote in his original Gospel, scholars compare the various manuscripts of Luke. In the great majority of cases, the wording of the manuscripts is the same. So in these cases, scholars can be certain that the copies are closely following Luke's original text. In some cases, however, there are differences.

Usually these differences are minor. In Luke 8:26, for example, some manuscripts read "the territory of the Gerasenes," others read "the territory of the Gadarenes," and still others, "the territory of the Gergesenes." In this case, scholars have judged that "Gerasenes" was most likely in

Luke's original, and the other variant readings came about due to intentional or unintentional changes by the copyists.

Consider Luke 23:17 as another example. It reads, "He was obliged to release one prisoner for them at the festival." This statement forms part of the narrative in which the crowd chooses between releasing Jesus or Barabbas. The verse is not printed in the main portion of the New American Bible (NAB) text (one popular translation), but rather is given only in a footnote. As the NAB note explains, it was most likely not part of Luke's original Gospel, because the verse is not found in many early and important Greek manuscripts. This detail, then, was apparently added by a copyist who was familiar with similar statements in Mark 15:6 or Matthew 27:15.

This process of attempting to reconstruct the original text of any book of the Bible is known as textual criticism. Scholars from around the world have cooperated in systematically comparing manuscripts stored in various libraries or museums. When differences occur, they make careful judgments, based on a variety of factors including the age and quality of the manuscripts, as to which reading is more likely to be original.

As a result of textual criticism, modern readers can have a high degree of certainty that our translations are based on Greek, Hebrew, or Aramaic texts that are essentially the same as the originals written thousands of years ago. In fact, modern readers can be more certain that we are reading the original text than at any other time since the texts were first copied. Earlier translators had to rely on the few manuscripts that they happened to have, many of which were relatively recent copies or of poor quality. In contrast, today scholars have access to thousands of carefully preserved manuscripts. Many of these have been discovered within the past sixty years, including the Dead Sea scrolls for Old Testament criticism and important New Testament papyri. Finally, the methods of textual criticism have been greatly improved and refined in the past century as well.

English Translations of the Bible

Once one has come as close as possible to the original Hebrew, Aramaic, or Greek text of a biblical book, one still has the task of translating from that original language into English. Let's take a look at some of the history of that process.

The first translation of the Bible into English is associated with the work of John Wycliffe (1330–1384). Wycliffe and associates worked from Latin translations, completing a first edition around 1382.

The first English translation from the original Hebrew, Aramaic, and Greek was made by William Tyndale during the upheavals of the Protestant Reformation. Tyndale's early plans at translation were blocked in his native England. He moved to Germany, where he was influenced by Martin Luther's translations and theology. His English New Testament translation was published in 1526 and copies smuggled back into England. English authorities, fearing Lutheran influence and accusing Tyndale of inaccurate translations, banned his writings. Tyndale himself was eventually imprisoned and executed in 1536.

He remains the single most important figure in the history of English translations of the Bible; the majority of the wording of the famous King James Version follows Tyndale.

A series of translations based on Tyndale's work followed, but most were now completed under the official patronage of the Church of England (first led by King Henry VIII). These revisions culminated in the King James Version (KJV) published in 1611. The KJV is universally recognized as a masterpiece of English prose and was the standard English Bible for more than two centuries. It is still widely used today, especially in some conservative Christian circles. In 1982, the New King James Version was published, updating the Elizabethan language of the KJV.

The Tyndale–King James tradition of translation continued. From 1881–1885, the Revised Version (RV) of the KJV, authorized by the Church of England, but completed in cooperation with other Protestant churches, was published. A further revision of this work by American scholars was published as the American Standard Version (ASV) in 1901. The Revised Standard Version (RSV), a further revision of the ASV, was published from 1946 to 1956; it was updated as the New Revised Standard Version (NRSV) in 1989.

Many other American versions were published in the twentieth century. Among the most noteworthy: the New International Version (NIV) produced by a team of evangelical scholars (1978); the Jewish Publication Society's 1985 translation (NJPS); and the Good News Bible in Today's English Version (TEV), published from 1966–1979 and updated in 1992, now known as the Good News Translation (GNT). These recent translations were an attempt at a fresh translation of the Bible into modern English apart from the Tyndale–King James tradition.

Roman Catholic Translations

For many years, Bibles in the Roman Catholic tradition were translations of the Vulgate, an ancient Latin translation of the Bible that was accorded official status by the Council of Trent (1546). The standard English translation was the Douay-Rheims version, first published in the early 1600s and revised in the mid 1700s by Bishop Challoner. Modern Catholic biblical translations began with Pope Pius XII's encyclical *Divino Afflante Spiritu,* issued in 1943, which called for translation from the original languages. Members of the Catholic Biblical Association of America began translation work the next year, culminating in 1970 with the publication of the New American Bible (NAB). The NAB New Testament was revised in 1987, and the Psalms were revised in 1991. Another popular American English version is the Jerusalem Bible (JB), first published in 1966 and revised in 1985 (NJB). These versions are inspired by La Bible de Jerusalem, a French translation produced at the École biblique in Jerusalem (revised version 1973). The Jerusalem Bible thus considers both the French translation as well as the original languages.

In accordance with the encouragement of the Vatican Council II decree *Dogmatic Constitution on Divine Revelation (Dei Verbum,* 1965), Catholics have been involved in ecumenical translation projects. Various traditionally Protestant translations now have Catholic editions: for example, the RSV Catholic edition (1966), the NRSV Catholic Edition (1989), and the Good News Translation with Deuterocanonicals, Second Edition (1992). Likewise, non-Catholic scholars were involved in both the original NAB translation and its revisions.

Translation Theories

Different translations have quite distinct goals. One basic distinction is between translations that strive for a formal equivalence and those that strive for a dynamic equivalence.

The formal-equivalence approach is a more literal one. It strives to stay close to the vocabulary, structure, and even word order of the original Hebrew, Aramaic, or Greek. The goal is to allow the reader who does not know these languages to gain some sense of the original wording. The NAB and versions in the Tyndale–King James tradition follow this basic approach.

The formal-equivalence approach, furthermore, allows one to retain traditional biblical and liturgical vocabulary and phrasing. Certain traditional word choices such as justification, righteousness, and salvation have become fixed in English theological discourse, and it might well be confusing simply to drop them in favor of other, more modern words or phrases.

Finally, the formal-equivalence approach allows for a formal, dignified reading that is more appropriate for proclamation in worship services. This liturgical concern was a major guiding factor in the decisions of the NAB translators.

In contrast, a dynamic-equivalence approach attempts to recast the meaning of the original language in natural, modern English, with little regard for the structure or specific vocabulary of the original language. This is the approach taken in the GNT. The extreme end of the dynamic-equivalence spectrum is the paraphrase—an approach that is no longer a true translation but simply an attempt to convey the main points of the original language into the new language. One of the best known English paraphrase translations is The Message Remix: The Bible in Contemporary Language, by Eugene H. Peterson, a work published from 1993 to 2003.

An example illustrates the different approaches. In the formal-equivalence tradition, the NRSV refers to a man who owed "ten thousand talents" in its translation of one of Jesus' parables (Mt 18:24). This is a literal rendering of the Greek monetary unit *talanton*. Using the dynamic-equivalent approach, the GNT interprets this in modern English as "millions of dollars." The NAB simply translates "a huge amount."

The different approaches of these various translations reveals the need for a translation to be accompanied by further explanations, both in the form of notes that accompany the actual text and in the form of introductory essays (the NAB uses both forms). In combining the formal-equivalence approach with explanatory notes and essays, the NAB seeks to allow the reader (1) access to the vocabulary, structure, and meaning of the original language, and (2) access to the meaning of the biblical text in a way that is comprehensible for modern English speakers.

Another translation issue arises from the fact that our society today is more sensitive to the use of language that might exclude certain groups. The NRSV revision of the RSV, for example, employs gender-inclusive language. The NAB revision of the New Testament and the Psalms is more inclusive, dropping the use of *man* as a generic reference to all humans. The NAB New Testament does however retain the use of the pronouns he and his to correspond with the use of anyone or everyone, and continues using the term brothers as a translation of the Greek *adelphoi*—a term of address that is masculine in form but whose range of meaning certainly included both men and women.

In 1992, the United States Conference of Catholic Bishops (USCCB) approved the use of the revised NAB in the new *Lectionary for Mass* (the book of official readings for use in Catholic worship). Vatican officials raised some objections, primarily to the use of inclusive language. In the Vatican's view, some inclusive translations were not faithful to the original meaning of the text and dropping traditional phrases such as Son of Man would result in a loss of theological meaning. A revised *Lectionary for Mass* (avoiding the controversial inclusive language and not using the revised Book of Psalms at all) was approved by the Vatican and the USCCB in 1997. As a result, there are differences in translation between the Roman Catholic Lectionary and the NAB translation of the Bible.

Martin Albl, PhD
Associate Professor
of Religious Studies
Presentation College
Aberdeen, South Dakota

Reading the Bible: Tools for Understanding

Getting Started

Picking up the Bible may be a new experience for some, so knowing how to navigate its pages is important. This library of sorts, many books within the covers of a single work, is divided into two main parts that reflect the historical evolution of Judaism and Christianity: the Old Testament, known to Judaism as the Tanak, and the New Testament. Each of these sections has a number of individual books. To locate a particular passage within the Scriptures, three pieces of information are necessary: the name of the book, the chapter, and the particular verse(s)—e.g., John 3:16–17. In this example from the New Testament, John is the name of the book, 3 is the chapter number, and 16 and 17 are the designated verses.

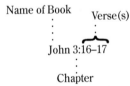

Name of Book

Verse(s)

John 3:16–17

Chapter

In order to read the Bible well, it is also important to understand how the footnotes and cross-references function. Depending on the translation, the footnotes may provide information about a variety of issues, including cultural and ritual practices, definitions of unique terminology, information about individuals or their roles in society, and so on. Cross-references to verses in other parts of the Bible can be very help-

ful. They indicate recurring themes, they can connect the New Testament with the Old Testament, and they can demonstrate a particular author's dependence on other works in the Bible, to name only a few uses. Neither the footnotes nor the cross-references are part of the ancient Bible text. Rather, they are added to an English translation of the Bible by modern biblical scholars to help readers better understand the Bible.

Two-Part Story: The Old and New Testaments

Christians traditionally refer to the first part of the Bible as the Old Testament. The word testament means "covenant" or "agreement." This reference makes sense only in relation to the Christian Scriptures that have as their second part the New Testament, referring to the New Covenant in Jesus Christ. Before the beginning of Christianity, and still today, the works that Christians call the Old Testament belong to the sacred texts of Judaism.

Jewish people use the Hebrew word Tanak to describe their Bible. The word is an acronym derived from the three major parts of the Hebrew Bible (these works were originally written in Hebrew): the Torah (meaning law or instructions), Nevi'im (meaning prophets), and Kethuvim (meaning writings). The heart and center of the Old Testament is the Torah (Hebrew), also known as the Pentateuch (Greek). It is composed of the first five books of the Bible: Genesis, Exodus, Leviticus, Numbers, and Deuteronomy. The Pentateuch recalls God's Covenant established with the Hebrew people, God's call and the Exodus of the Hebrew people from slavery in Egypt, and God's Law given to the Hebrew people through Moses to help them grow in their relationship with God and as a community as they stand poised to enter the Promised Land.

The prophetic writings (Nevi'im) include the former prophets: Joshua, Judges, 1 and 2 Samuel, and 1 and 2 Kings. The later prophets are also known as the writing prophets, and their works include Isaiah, Jeremiah, Ezekiel, and the book of the twelve (called the minor prophets): Hosea, Joel, Amos, Obadiah, Jonah, Micah, Nahum, Habakkuk, Zephaniah, Haggai, Zechariah, and Malachi.

The writings (Kethuvim) include the wisdom book of Job and the poetic books of Psalms, Proverbs, Ecclesiastes, and the Song of Songs. It also includes Ruth, 1 and 2 Chronicles, Ezra, Nehemiah, Esther, Lamentations, and Daniel.

So far this listing of accepted books of the Hebrew Scriptures referred to as the canon is the same for Jews, Protestants, and Catholics. The word canon comes from the Greek for "reed" or "straight stick," meaning that by which something is measured. It refers to the list of writings that are recognized by a religious community as authoritative in defining and teaching its core beliefs. However, the Roman Catholic Church follows the canon derived from a later Greek version of the Hebrew Scriptures known as the Septuagint. This list includes several additional works collectively referred to as deuterocanonical, in other words belonging to a second or later canon. This term is applied to books of the Bible whose place in the canon was at some time denied or doubted in the Church. The deuterocanonical books are Tobit, Judith, 1 and 2 Maccabees, Sirach (or Ecclesiasticus), the Book of Wisdom, and portions of Daniel and Esther. (See "What Is the Bible?").

The second major division of the Bible is the New Testament. It was written in the same kind of Greek (koine, which was a common or universal language used throughout the Middle East, versus classical Greek) as the Septuagint. The New Testament canon, composed of twenty-seven books, is identical for Catholics and Protestants. There are four Gospels: Matthew, Mark, Luke, and John. The Gospels, meaning "good news," tell the story of the ministry, death, and Resurrection of Jesus Christ. Although the origin of the gospel genre is unclear, early Christians used it to good effect to proclaim their faith in Jesus, whom they believed to be the Christ, the Messiah of God.

The author of the Gospel of Luke actually wrote a two-part narrative that included the Gospel and the Acts of the Apostles. Acts reveals the origin of the early Christian community

> **The word *canon* comes from the Greek for "reed" or "straight stick," meaning that by which something is measured. It refers to the list of writings that are recognized by a religious community as authoritative in defining and teaching its core beliefs.**

that formed immediately after the Resurrection and Ascension of Jesus. Acts narrates critical episodes in the lives of the early Christians and highlights the actions of Peter and Paul.

There are two other types of writing that appear in the New Testament—letters or epistles, and an apocalypse. There are twenty-one letters ascribed to leaders of the early Christian community. Paul and his disciples wrote the first set of letters. There are seven others that are attributed to Peter, James, Jude, and John.

The Book of Revelation is the last book of the New Testament. Though it was not the final book written, its placement in the canon is appropriate for it is concerned with the last things.

Given the number and the varied style of books that appear within the covers of the Bible, it is essential to have tools for interpretation and study.

Tools for Biblical Study Included in This Guide

In addition to the several articles you have just read on historical, cultural, literary, translation, ecclesiastical, theological, and other issues related to an informed reading of the Bible, this guide includes other articles and aids to enhance understanding for college students or others involved in introductory Scripture or theology courses:

- An introduction to each section of the Bible. Written in accessible language, these introductions provide scholarly information related to the major divisions in both the Old and New Testaments.

- A timeline presenting human history and biblical history. Understanding the historical setting for each of the biblical books provides the reader with clearer insight regarding the meaning of particular books or passages.

- Maps that correspond to the historical framework of the biblical books. Knowing the lay of the land can enhance interpretation and cultural knowledge and therefore provide greater understanding. For example, a realization that the Fertile Crescent area was a coveted land because it ensured survival is good to know when examining the number of wars fought by the Israelites.

- A glossary of terms for understanding particular terminology related to biblical studies. This glossary can be supplemented by the use of Bible dictionaries, which are widely available and easy to use.

- A number of charts. These provide the reader with quick references to key information, people, and places in the Bible.

Additional Resources for Biblical Study

Besides what is available in this Bible guide, there are many other resources that can be helpful in your study of the Bible. Most are available in your local library, many you can find online, and some you may want to purchase for your own library. We will mention just a few here.

Bible Dictionaries

As commonplace as a dictionary might seem, it is an invaluable tool. A Bible dictionary provides a wealth of information for the user. The terminology that is defined is drawn almost exclusively from the Scriptures. The definitions explain the meaning of biblical terms as they were understood in their historical and cultural contexts.

Some Bible dictionaries offer only the essential, sometimes brief, definition of a term; others provide complete essays that explore the word in much greater depth, like an encyclopedia. Given the way that words can change in meaning over time and in different parts of the world, even among different writers, a few of the larger Bible dictionaries help the user to understand a word as it specifically pertains to the biblical passage where it is found.

Bible dictionaries are a critical resource for appropriately interpreting the Bible. Consider, for example, the meaning of the term *Pharisee*. Because the Pharisees frequently appear in the Gospels as the opponents of Jesus and his ministry, one might conclude that they are the bad guys. However, in fact, they were considered to be experts in right interpretation of the Jewish Torah and people looked up to them as the models of Jewish holiness. Understanding the history of the Pharisaic movement within Judaism and their role in the life of first-century Jews is critical for a balanced assessment of the Gospel writers' portrayal of the Pharisees' actions in relation to Jesus.

Concordances

Another important tool for biblical study is the concordance. A concordance provides an alphabetical listing of words found in the Bible with references to the passages where they appear. A concordance can be helpful in finding a specific scriptural text. For example, if you were searching for the verse, "You are the salt of the earth" (Mt 5:13), you could look up salt in the concordance and that would lead you to all the places in the Bible where this word is found. Of course, to use a concordance effectively, you need to develop the skill of selecting a word from the biblical quotation that is most likely to lead you to the correct citation. Because most people will be reading the Bible in translation, not in its original languages of Hebrew, Aramaic, and Greek, they need to use a concordance that is keyed to their translation, such as NAB, NRSV, or another. This information is usually included on the title page of the concordance.

Bible Commentaries

Bible commentaries are essential resources for biblical study. They appear in a variety of formats, some as a single-volume work and others as multivolume sets. The most detailed commentaries are those that treat a single book of the Bible rather than several books at once. Biblical commentaries contain a gold mine of information drawn from the comments of biblical scholars. They are designed to help the user move through individual books of the Bible section by section, offering a wealth of information for interpretation.

Commentaries explore many dimensions of a biblical book, including literary forms, historical context, cultural and ritual practices, and the theological perspectives of the author and final redactors (or editors) of the text. After addressing some introductory questions like authorship, date of composition, and the audience to which the book was originally addressed, a commentary divides the biblical book according to logical segments or pericopes (short passages from a written work) and provides a detailed, often verse-by-verse, commentary on the meaning of the text.

When selecting a biblical commentary, it is important to consider the background of the biblical scholar and his or her purpose for writing. Some commentaries are written with a particular faith tradition in mind, for example, an audience that consists of Protestant evangelical Christians or Roman Catholics. These commentaries will differ from one another in their conclusions about the meaning of a particular biblical text because their authors have differing understandings of inspiration and different methods of biblical interpretation. Other commentaries do not address issues of faith at all. Instead, the biblical scholar provides historical and cultural background and analyzes the literary features of a biblical text, but leaves it to the reader to make contemporary applications for faith. Whatever the approach, you also need to know that the author has the academic preparation to write a credible commentary, namely, advanced training (usually a doctorate) in biblical studies. Often this information is included in the preface or on the jacket cover of the book.

Online Resources

A final comment regarding online resources—students often make the mistake of accepting any or all material found on the Internet as credible and relevant. Unfortunately this is not the case. When you buy and read hard copy books (print media), you can be relatively secure about the quality of the work because book editors and publishers screen the materials they publish. However, when it comes to the Internet, people can write and publish whatever they want, without having to demonstrate that they have the academic credentials to do so. Therefore, you need to be especially careful about checking the academic training of online authors of biblical commentaries. Occasionally, you will find Web sites that have online versions of hard copy books or commentaries that were written by biblical scholars. However, because of copyright restrictions, most of these books are at least seventy-five years old. Since biblical scholarship continues to develop, and in fact has made tremendous strides in the past twenty-five years, it is important to employ current and relevant resources for biblical interpretation. There is good information available on the Internet, but it is important to identify when the material was published and by whom.

Shannon Schrein, OSF, PhD
Professor and Chair
of Religious Studies
Lourdes College
Sylvania, Ohio

Understanding the Major Sections of the Bible

· *The Old Testament* ·

Introduction to the Pentateuch

Background

The Hebrew Bible or Old Testament took shape over many centuries. Long before the final written form of the Scriptures came to be, bits and pieces of it were told orally, sometimes as stories, sometimes in worship rituals, sometimes as legal judgments about particular disputed claims. In time, these oral traditions, long passed down by word of mouth, were codified in written form as stories, liturgies, and legal texts. Finally, after many rewrites and much editing, the Old Testament emerged as the Sacred Scriptures divided into three sections. The first and most authoritative section of the Bible for most Jews is called the Torah, a Hebrew word often translated as "law"

or "the Law." The second and third sections of the Hebrew Scriptures are called the Prophets and the Writings, respectively. Hints of this three-part canon of the Scriptures were found in the foreword of Sirach (Ecclesiasticus) around 180 BCE and later in the New Testament (Mt 5:17, Lk 14:44, Jn 1:45), but the roots of this division go back much earlier. As the canon of the Scriptures evolved over time, and with the inclusion of additional books, the Old Testament canon as we know it was divided differently (for more information, see the article "What Is the Bible?").

Torah: The Heart of the Old Testament

The Torah is considered the heart of

the Old Testament, as the Gospels are the heart of the New Testament. The term Torah can also be understood more broadly than simply "law" or even a set of laws. Its meaning includes general instructions or teaching, including the story or narrative into which these instructions or laws are sometimes placed. Law, instruction, teaching, and story are all found in the Torah of the Scriptures, that is, the first five books of the Bible known to non-Hebrew readers as the Books of Genesis, Exodus, Leviticus, Numbers, and Deuteronomy. As the Hebrew Scriptures were translated into Greek, the name for this first and most sacred part of the Scriptures became known by its Greek title, "The Pentateuch," meaning, "the five books."

The Torah or Pentateuch opens with the story of Creation and concludes with the death and mourning of one of its central characters, Moses. It opens with stories of the world's formation and closes with the children and grandchildren of freed Hebrew slaves standing on the banks of the Jordan River waiting to enter the Promised Land. In between, stories are told of the faith and disobedience of the ancestors, the escape from Egyptian slavery, the giving of the Ten Commandments on Mount Sinai, forty years of wandering to and fro in the desert, and several significant law codes woven throughout.

If one reads the stories of the Torah or the Pentateuch according to the chronology laid out in the stories themselves, it becomes apparent that the storytellers wished to emphasize certain parts of the story over others. For example, the first fifty chapters of the Pentateuch, the Book of Genesis, purports to cover about 2,300 years,

according to the narrative's own internal chronology. We now know, of course, that in actual historical time, such a time frame is much too short, giving us a clue to the writer's ancient mythic worldview. The next part of the story, which tells of the Exodus from Egypt and the giving of the Law and other events at Sinai, takes eighty-one chapters (Exodus, Leviticus, and Numbers chaps. 1 through 14) to tell about events that cover just over one year! The last twenty-two chapters of Numbers cover the forty years of wandering in the wilderness. Finally, the Book of Deuteronomy spends thirty-four chapters recounting the last day or two in Moses' life as he interprets the Law for a new generation on the banks of the Jordan River, in what appears to be his last will and testament. Given such a contrived chronological storytelling structure, clearly, for the storytellers of the Pentateuch, the Exodus experience and the giving of the Law at Sinai were critically important. These two experiences provide a lens through which all other experiences before and after were to be understood. In the central themes of salvation and covenant, grace and obligation, gospel and law, freedom and commitment found throughout the Scriptures, one sees traces of the Exodus and Sinai traditions.

When Moses is called to lead the Hebrew slaves from Egypt, the Lord promises not only to "rescue them from the hands of the Egyptians" but also to "lead them out of that land into a good and spacious land" inhabited by other peoples (Ex 3:8). More than one hundred and fifty times in the Pentateuch, the ancestors of Israel are not only promised many descendants, a relationship with God, and that they will be a blessing to the whole world, but they are also promised a new homeland. Genesis 12:1–3 provides the most succinct expression of these promises made by the Lord to Abram. As if to underscore these promises, the earliest oral confessions of faith recorded in the Scriptures (e.g., Dt 6:20–24, 26:5–9) also recount the fulfillment of these promises in one form or another, especially the promise of a new homeland.

If good stories have good endings, then the Torah or Pentateuch seems to end all too abruptly. Given how many times a homeland was promised throughout the rest of the Pentateuch, one might have expected that a good storyteller would have ended the Torah story with the people having arrived in their new homeland. They certainly had available to them stories of glorious conquest and entrance into the land as told in the Book of Joshua. Indeed, one might have guessed that the Book of Joshua would have been the most natural conclusion to the story as it unfolds in the Pentateuch. Why not a hexateuch (six books), then, instead of a Pentateuch (five books)? Why does the story end as it does with Moses dead and the fate of the ancestors in limbo? Why does the Pentateuch, the heart of the Old Testament, end with a landless people standing on the banks of the Jordan River looking longingly across to the Promised Land? Why, then, does the Pentateuch seem to end so badly? It's as if, in terms of the stories of Jesus in the New Testament, the Gospel writers would have told of Jesus' birth, life, teachings, and death, but left out the most important part—his Resurrection! The ending of the Pentateuch, then, comes as a near total surprise.

Something must have happened in the intervening years between the first telling of these old, old stories about the promises God made to the ancestors and the final version of their telling in the Pentateuch that deliberately leaves out the fulfillment of those promises, especially the promise of land, as told in the Book of Joshua. Indeed, something huge did happen many years later, which provides the best explanation for why the Pentateuch ends the way it does and suggests a relative time frame for dating when the Pentateuch was finally compiled.

The Exile Factor

We now know that the Hebrew Bible, after a long process of gathering and editing oral and written sources, began to emerge in its final form during and soon after the People of God once again found themselves as refugees in the Babylonian Exile (587–538 BCE). Their great Temple, their land, their kingdom, indeed, everything that had given them a sense of identity and destiny for some six hundred years, was all gone. If you imagine these refugees standing now on the banks of the Tigris and Euphrates Rivers in Babylon (modern-day Iraq), looking longingly eastward toward their homeland back over the Jordan River, the Torah story ending where it ends must have sounded like good news, wonderful news, of the possibility of an imminent homecoming. The Jordan River could well have been the Tigris and Euphrates Rivers of Babylon. The hills of Moab overlooking the Promised Land, where Moses and the people spend their last days together as described at the end of the Pentateuch, could well have been the fertile crescent of Babylon where the people find themselves now hearing the Pentateuch story in its final form.

The emotions of those who heard the Pentateuch read aloud for the first time, either in the Babylonian captivity or soon thereafter, are captured in the story of Ezra, the great scribe. In the Book of Nehemiah (8:1, 9–12), Ezra reads "the book of the law (or Torah) of Moses" to the returning refugees in the square of the Water Gate in Jerusalem. The people all stand in reverence throughout the reading, which took all morning. When the people hear the words of the Law (Torah) read, they weep (8:9). Soon after the reading and with a little encouragement from Ezra, their weeping turns to great rejoicing. If only reading the Torah or Pentateuch still evoked such awe and depth of emotion.

All readers, in some sense, must enter the story of the Pentateuch, first and foremost, from the perspective of those first hearers and readers. All readers now read it, as it were, backward from the Exile. Now, as it was heard by the refugees in Babylon, all the stories and characters of the Torah or Pentateuch become larger than life, bigger than history, archetypal in force. In the Pentateuch the characters and events are more than historical. They have become mythic in revelatory power.

Now, the fact that the Pentateuch opens in the Garden of Eden located in Babylon between the waters of the Tigris and Euphrates Rivers matters. The first humans in the opening chapters of the Book of Genesis are invited to make choices of life-altering consequence just as the people gathered around Moses at the end of the Book of Deuteronomy face choices for blessing or cursing, for life or death. Reading such stories from the perspective of the Babylonian Exile or any existential exile, for that matter, becomes a new invitation to appreciate how one's destiny is shaped by one's choices. Adam and Eve were exiled from Eden for having made wrong choices.

Indeed, the stories in the second part of the Hebrew Bible, the Former Prophets (Joshua through 2 Kings), recount the choices of consequence that were made by all those who first entered the Promised Land from the banks of the Jordan River. Those choices eventually led them once again out of the Promised Land into exile, first to Assyria, then to Babylon. Ironically, the Book of Joshua, which would seemingly have fit best as the climax of the Pentateuch, has now been placed, instead, as the introduction to a negative history of choices gone wrong that lead to exile. The beginning and ending of the Pentateuch are bookends of choice and its consequence.

The primeval stories that tell of Adam, Eve, the serpent, the great flood, and the Tower of Babel in Genesis chapters 1 through 11 are more than origin stories per se. When read together, as a whole, these stories might legitimately be called a theo-political manifesto composed by a people living as subjects beneath the coercive power of Babylon. Each biblical story seems to have near parallels to Babylonian origin stories only

> **All readers, in some sense, must enter the story of the Pentateuch, first and foremost, from the perspective of those first hearers and readers.**

now retold so as to be critical of the domination system of the Babylonian city-state. Later, in the Book of Exodus, the stories of the Lord defeating the empire of an unnamed pharaoh allow for mythic comparison to any empire that tries to subjugate God's People. Clearly, from the perspective of the Pentateuch, bondage in Babylon need not be any more permanent than bondage in Egypt had been. The extended story of Joseph living in exile in Egypt not only serves as a paradigm for how a person of minority status might manage to become a "light to the nations" but also how the people might benefit from a Nehemiah-like leader who later becomes influential in Persian empire politics. The Pentateuch, throughout, has a strong bias against empire politics, while at the same time offering pragmatic illustrative stories for how a minority people living under the control of empire might survive until their promised liberation. The Pentateuch, as such, might be considered subversive literature on a par with the underground literature of dissident playwrights.

The stories of Adam and Eve suffering only exile from Eden and not immediate death, of Cain's exile to the East of Eden being a sort of protective custody from his avengers, and of God starting Creation all over again with Noah in spite of ongoing human sinfulness are heard in fresh ways by people who are on the brink of starting over again in their own exile. Exile may not be an ending but a beginning. Indeed, Abraham and Sarah, whose story begins in Babylon, immediately following the Tower of Babel mess, offer renewed hope for all would-be refugees. Abraham became the mythic father of faith for the world's three dominant monothe-

istic religions, precisely because in his refugee status he had to learn to live by faith in a stateless, boundaryless existence, relying only on God for his identity and existence. He and Sarah were called to leave Babylon in order to live a life of exile, that of travelers toward the Promised Land of Canaan. Even after they arrive there, they leave almost immediately, into exile again only this time in Egypt because of famine. As life was for Abraham and Sarah, so is life for those living in seemingly permanent exile in Babylon. Their confessions proclaimed: "My father was a wandering Aramean" (Dt 26:5). Perhaps, wandering like Abraham, even in the wilderness for forty years as they would later do, was survivable with God on their side. Perhaps, they could even begin to imagine that they, like Abraham and Sarah, were once again being called out of Babylon to go to the Land of Promise (Is 51:2).

Abraham's grandson Jacob, renamed Israel on his way into exile to Haran (Babylon), receives his new name and renewed promises of destiny even as he flees for his life from his murderous brother Esau. Jacob, now Israel, eventually returns to the Promised Land in humility, bearing gifts and bowing down before his brother in reconciliation. Recounting such a tale would remind those returning, or about to return, to Judah from Babylon of the need to consider how delicate any rapprochement with those living back in the homeland might need to be.

In Exile: Maintaining Communities of Faith

The law codes and legal material found throughout the Pentateuch serve to remind people living in exile of the importance that worship and ethics play in the formation and maintenance of communities of faith and life. Indeed, people living in exile might easily be tempted to assimilate to the dominant culture, choose the gods of the empire, and too easily forget the Covenant relationship promised to them by God. All the various versions of the Law in the Pentateuch seem to function less as stories telling of Israel's past, than as stories creating an imagined future around profound jurisprudence and constitutional formation. Ultimately, the variety of laws in the Pentateuch, and especially those that have been explicitly updated from earlier versions of the Law such as Moses models in the Book of Deuteronomy, suggest that even these sacred laws may be in need of periodic revision. The laws serve as a summons to the people to live lives of obedience and true worship, to make choices for blessing, now more than ever, as they stand on the banks of the Jordan or Tigris and Euphrates Rivers, living in hope of yet-to-be-fulfilled promises.

When Jesus is asked by some lawyerly peers who are trying to test his faith, "Which commandment in the law is the greatest?" (Mt 22:34–40), he responds with two verses from the Pentateuch. First, he quotes Deuteronomy 6:5: "You shall love the Lord, your God, with all your heart, and with all your soul, and with all your mind" (verse 37). Jesus adds that "this is the greatest and the first commandment" (verse 38). Second, he quotes Leviticus 19:18: "The second is like it: You shall love your neighbor as yourself" (verse 39). Jesus concludes by saying, "The whole law [meaning Torah or Pentateuch in this instance] and the prophets depend on these two commandments" (verse 40). In a sense, in reciting these two verses from the Pentateuch, Jesus responds to two questions asked by the Lord at the beginning of the Pentateuch. To Adam and Eve hiding in shame because of their disobedience, the Lord seeks them out and asks, "Where are you?" (Gn 3:9). To Cain, after he kills his brother, the Lord asks, "Where is your brother?" (Gn 4:9). The first question invites reflection on one's relationship to God, the Creator. The second question invites reflection on one's sister or brother or neighbor. In short, Jesus' summary of the Law is a summary of the Pentateuch—love God and love others!

James E. Brenneman, PhD
President of Goshen College
Goshen, Indiana

Introduction to the Historical Books

Background

Some people are prevented from reading the Historical Books because they find history dull or pointless. They share Huckleberry Finn's attitude to historical study: "I don't put no stock in dead people." However, the same people who say they find history dull find great enjoyment in other forms of storytelling, such as novels, television, movies, and gossip. Why, then, does history stand accused of being boring? Perhaps only a certain understanding of history is at fault. Modern people tend to think of historical narratives strictly as accounts of what actually happened in the past. Even a cursory reading of the Bible's historical narratives, however, should reveal that the biblical writers did not share this view.

Biblical Narratives versus Modern History

Biblical narratives differ from modern historical (or even fiction) writing in several respects. One striking difference is that biblical writers make extensive use of composed speeches and dialogue. Modern historians rarely include speeches in their narratives unless they have reliable access to the exact spoken words of persons who lived in the past. Biblical writers, however, like other ancient historians, abided by different conventions in the narration of history. Although they also lacked reliable access to spoken words, they regularly composed speeches to add interest to their narratives and highlight the issues at stake in the events (e.g.,

Jos chap. 23, 1 Sm 8:10–18, 1 Kgs 8:22–64).

Because modern historians do not often make use of dialogue, they resort to other literary devices to add color to their histories. For example, they sometimes supply detailed descriptions of landscape and character sketches that profile the temperament, attitudes, and values of individuals important to the story. By contrast, biblical writers rarely provide descriptive details concerning the landscape, buildings, or people unless these details are important to the narrative.

In fact, the biblical writers rarely give the reader access to the internal life of characters. We are left to infer character thoughts and motives from their words and actions. This reticence frequently creates ambiguity. For example, in 2 Samuel, the motive for Ahithophel's suicide is not provided (17:23). Does he kill himself because he is overly concerned about his failing reputation or because he knows that, once his advice is ignored, David will regain the throne and punish those who sided with Absalom?

Modern historians often make explicit judgments about the actions of the people they describe. Even though many people think of the Bible as moralistic, biblical writers rarely state explicitly whether an action was good or bad. For instance, the several suicides in biblical narrative occur without narrative comment, so that interpreters may disagree about whether the Old Testament prohibits suicide (Jgs 9:52–54, 16:25–30;

1 Sm 31:4–5; 2 Sm 17:23; 1 Kgs 16:15–20). Most often, moral evaluations are placed in the mouths of other characters (2 Sm 13:12–13). The major exception to this rule is the regular evaluation of kings as good or bad according to their obedience to the Law (1 Kgs 15:34).

Illuminating the past to understand the present. The biblical narrative employs engaging storytelling about the past in order to understand the present. The past is illuminating because events have a way of recurring. We can gain insight into our present situation not only by understanding how it developed from past events but also by searching for past situations analogous to our own. Biblical narrative employs extensive use of analogy to indicate the commonalities among diverse events. These similarities invite the reader to consider historical patterns and to discern what is unique in each episode.

For instance, the crime at Gibeah (Jgs chap. 19) connects with several other narratives. In the story, the men of Gibeah want to rape the male guest who is staying with one of their neighbors. To avoid this crime, the male guest thrusts his concubine outside for the men to gang rape through the night. In the morning, he finds her body on the doorstep, takes her corpse home, cuts it into twelve pieces, and sends the parts to the twelve tribes of Israel in an attempt to mobilize the tribes to exact revenge for the crime. Most obvious, the outrage at Gibeah is strikingly reminiscent of the attempted rape at Sodom (Gn chap. 19), in which the men of the city want to rape the male guests of Lot. Although Lot offers his daughters as substitute victims

for his guests in Genesis chapter 19, the guests are angels who save themselves and Lot's family from the crowd. Through the many connections between the stories, Gibeah is presented as an Israelite city that is as bad as the proverbial wicked city of Sodom (Is 1:9–10, 3:9; Jer 23:14). The magnitude of the crime is adequate cause for the civil war that follows. Gibeah, which is the hometown of Saul (1 Sm 10:26, 11:4), stands in contrast to Bethlehem (Jgs 19:1–2), the hometown of David (1 Sm chap. 16), and to Jebus, a Canaanite city that will later be known as Jerusalem (Jgs 19:10). The outrage at Gibeah leads the Israelite tribes to nearly extinguish the tribe of Benjamin after the Levite sends the twelve parts of his concubine's body among the tribes of Israel to raise an army (Jgs 19:29–30). Later, Saul will send parts of oxen among the tribes to raise an Israelite army (1 Sm 11:4–8). The connections among these stories invite the reader to consider the stories together. Among the implications is a comparison between David and Saul. David is the better man (1 Sm 15:28) who comes from the better city. Saul, meanwhile, has a dubious heritage for a king (1 Sm 9:21).

Perhaps the most obvious reason to read the Historical Books is to learn about Israel's past. However, one can fairly ask whether this history can best be learned from the biblical accounts or from books written by modern scholars with such titles as *A History of Ancient Israel.* Modern historians have access to information that is not mentioned in the biblical texts, such as ancient inscriptions found in and around the land of Israel. Also, we think of modern historical works as somehow objective in a way that ancient narratives are not.

Consequently, a modern book might be a more accurate guide to Israel's history than the biblical books.

Fact or fiction. The first section in this introduction began the discussion of how ancient and modern historical narratives differ and how these differences reflect various ideas about what history is. Because modern historians often seek to present their work as objective and scientific, they avoid rhetorical techniques associated with imaginative or persuasive writing. Biblical narrative uses techniques common to imaginative and persuasive discourse (such as composed dialogues) because history is understood as an imaginative enterprise (representing the past) with a persuasive dimension.

Because the biblical narrative does use rhetoric in an imaginative effort to persuade, scholars disagree about how reliable the information derived from biblical narrative is. Consequently, they strive to separate the interpretations from the facts. The facts are difficult to establish with certainty because the Bible remains the only significant written source for the history of Israel. In order to gauge the historical accuracy of the biblical narrative, scholars seek to correlate biblical texts with archaeological evidence to determine whether or not the archaeology confirms the biblical account. These efforts have met with mixed and inconclusive results. For example, archaeologists have found that the gates of Hazor, Meggido, and Gezer, dating from Solomon's time, share nearly identical fortification patterns, suggesting centralized control. Since 1 Kings 9:15 credits Solomon with construction at these sites, scholars associated the archaeological finds with Solomon's activity.

Recently, however, some archaeologists have questioned that the gates date to Solomon's time and think they were erected at a later time. If this is so, then the Bible attributes to Solomon the work of a later king, which leads one to wonder how much of the biblical account of Solomon is exaggerated. Overall, the archaeological evidence concerning ancient Israel does not offer the definitive proof of the Bible's historicity that some had hoped for. At the same time, several correlations between the Bible and archaeology and the biblical claims to historicity are not easily dismissed.

Biblical narrative (like other historical narrative) is not merely a passive presentation of historical facts but an imaginative presentation of Israel's history that seeks to persuade the reader of a given interpretation of that history. Historical information, however, can be interpreted in more than one way. Contemporary books with titles like *A History of Ancient Israel* narrate an interpretation of Israelite history that may or may not be similar to the interpretation of the biblical narrative. For example, the biblical narrative frequently involves the action of God in history, because it aims to reflect on Israel's relationship with God. God's activity, however, is beyond the scope of modern historical study. Therefore, modern histories of Israel (like modern histories of any other nation) make no reference to God as an agent in history. This significant difference between biblical and modern history necessarily leads modern historians to interpretations of Israel's history that may be at variance with the biblical version. Although modern histories are valuable for learning about the history of Israel and the history of the biblical text, all these historians, in varying degrees, use the Bible as a primary source. Consequently, anyone who wishes to learn about the history of ancient Israel should begin where the modern historians begin—with the biblical narrative.

What Are the Historical Books?

The Historical Books consist of the following biblical books: Joshua, Judges, Ruth, 1 and 2 Samuel, 1 and 2 Kings, 1 and 2 Chronicles, Ezra, Nehemiah, Tobit, Judith, Esther, and 1 and 2 Maccabees. Some of these books are more closely related to each other than others. Joshua, Judges, Samuel, and Kings together comprise a continuous narrative of Israel's history from the death of Moses until the end of the monarchy and the exile to Babylon. The Books of Chronicles, Ezra, and Nehemiah narrate a separate history of Israel that concludes with the reconstruction of Jerusalem after the return from the Babylonian Exile. The Books of Maccabees narrate partially parallel stories about the attempt of the Israelites to throw off the oppressive rule of the Greeks. Finally, Ruth, Tobit, Judith, and Esther are each short narratives that stand independently of each other and the other Historical Books (although Ruth is placed between Judges and 1 Samuel).

The first set of the Historical Books (Joshua to Kings) constitute the bulk of the historical material and are thought to be the most ancient of the various narratives. Although this narrative consists of several books, modern scholars believe that these books were edited together as one larger work known as the Deuteronomistic history. The Deuteronomistic history includes Deuteronomy, Joshua, Judges, Samuel, and Kings. This historical work is called "Deuteronomistic" because the whole history seems to be influenced by the language and thought of Deuteronomy. For instance, the Historical Books share Deuteronomy's view that worship should be centralized in Jerusalem (Dt 12:4–14; 1 Kgs 11:13,32,36; 2 Kgs 21:4,7; 23:27). The work seems to have incorporated earlier sources and edited them into a larger work narrating the history of Israel from Moses' final speech in the wilderness to the destruction of the Judean state and the exile of its leaders. Consequently, many scholars now approach these works as an interconnected whole rather than a disparate collection. The final editor gave shape and meaning to the whole narrative by composing several passages at significant moments. Some of these passages are narrative statements (Jgs chap. 2 and 2 Kgs chap. 17) while others are speeches placed in the mouths of major characters (Joshua in Jos chap. 23, Solomon in 1 Kgs chap. 8).

The Deuteronomistic history provides the most detailed history of Israel before the Exile. It begins with Moses' summary of the Law in Deuteronomy. The Book of Joshua narrates the conquest of the Promised Land under the leadership of Joshua. After Joshua's death, the period of the Judges begins. Although the Book of Judges ends before the birth of Samuel, the period of the monarchy does not begin until Samuel anoints the first king of Israel. During the reigns of Saul, David, and Solomon, the twelve tribes of Israel are unified under the rule of one king. After the death of Solomon, the period of the united monarchy ends and the divided monarchy begins when the northern tribes establish their own kingship apart from the dynasty of David. Ultimately, this northern kingdom is destroyed by the Assyrian Empire. Shortly afterward, the Babylonian Empire destroys the southern kingdom and forcibly removes its leading citizens to Babylon.

Among the Historical Books is another set of books related to one another. The work of the chronicler's history includes 1 and 2 Chronicles, Ezra, and Nehemiah. Scholars disagree about whether a single editor is responsible for all these books. However, the fact that the beginning of Ezra is the same as the end of 2 Chronicles indicates a connection between the works: Ezra and Nehemiah is the continuation of the history narrated in 1 and 2 Chronicles.

The Books of Chronicles draw on earlier sources (including the Deuteronomistic history) to narrate the history of Israel until the decree of Cyrus permitted the Jews to return from exile. Ezra and Nehemiah tell the history of Israel after this decree. In Chronicles, the description of events is sometimes significantly different from that of the Deuteronomistic history. For example, Chronicles shows little interest in the history of the northern kingdom of Israel that separated from the dynasty of David after the death of Solomon, whereas

Kings narrates the history of this kingdom in some detail. Comparison of these two histories will reveal many differences large and small.

Unlike the dual books of Samuel, Kings, and Chronicles, 1 and 2 Maccabees do not form a continuous narrative. Rather, each book relates some of the same history in different ways. These works tell the story of Israel from the conquest of Alexander the Great into the Maccabean period. The Maccabees were Jews who led a successful revolt against their Greek rulers and established Israel's independence until the Roman conquest.

The remaining Historical Books are sometimes characterized as short stories. They are Ruth, Tobit, Judith, and Esther. Each book is named after its main character. In three of the four cases, the main character is a woman who somehow saves Israel. Judith and Esther rescue Israel from the threat of destruction at enemy hands. Ruth, although a foreigner, saves an Israelite family from childlessness and becomes an ancestress of King David and therefore of Jesus. Finally, the book of Tobit narrates the suffering and redemption of two Israelite families living in exile.

David A. Bosworth, PhD
Professor of Old Testament Studies
Barry University
Miami Shores, Florida

Introduction to the Wisdom and Poetry Books

Background

Within each of us is a strong need to understand, to be able to make sense of life and of our own experiences. This desire to understand is inherent in our human makeup. It is apparent in children who constantly barrage their parents with questions. As we grow, our desire to know and to understand evolves with us. In today's world we have access to more information than we can possibly absorb in a lifetime. But it is more than knowledge that we seek. Our deeper need is genuine understanding—wisdom. Seeking wisdom and passing it on to others is an essential part of our lives.

Life is a sacred journey. For most of us the focus of the journey is finding meaning in our lives. For believers, faith serves as the prism through which we view life's experiences; thus it is faith seeking understanding (Saint Anselm's definition of theology) that propels us forward. The desire for wisdom is palpable for it is ultimately the desire for God. For Christians, our ancestors in the faith understood the need to grow in wisdom. They observed the patterns of life; questioned experiences, especially of suffering and death; and attempted to make sense of this sojourn on earth. Their wisdom, their questions, their observations are recorded in the wisdom tradition.

The wisdom writings comprise a cherished segment of the Hebrew Bible. The major works include Job, Proverbs, Ecclesiastes, Wisdom, and Sirach (also referred to as Ecclesiasticus). Two books, Psalms and the Song of Songs, reveal Israel's sacred songs. The Song of Songs, a love poem, contains echoes of wisdom themes and is placed in the canon in relation to the wisdom literature. Within the Psalter several individual psalms express wisdom themes and have been classified as such.

The most logical question to ask then is "What is wisdom?" Its definition is as varied as the works contained within the wisdom tradition. Wisdom connotes understanding the meaning of life. It also involves the instruction shared from one generation to the next. Wisdom implies a realization of the order of the universe and our place within it. It also recognizes the apparent randomness of life. Perhaps real wisdom comes when one realizes that wisdom can never be fully grasped in this life. Wisdom comes from seeking God. The search never ends, for the fullness of wisdom resides in God, who remains a mystery.

Themes in Wisdom Literature

What unifies these writings? What themes characterize these works? One common theme suggests that wisdom is discerned through observing human experiences and relationships. Fathers and mothers pass on to their children the wisdom gleaned from life in the hope that it will assist them in living in harmony with this world. In much the same way that parents today provide children with quips to guide behavior ("Eat your vegetables and you will grow up to be big and strong"; "If you can't say something nice, don't say anything at all"), the ancients offered proverbs intended to influence conduct: "When pride comes, disgrace comes; / but with the humble is wisdom" (Prv 11:2) and "Better a dry crust with peace / than a house full of feasting with strife" (Prv 17:1).

A second theme that appears frequently focuses on creation. Wisdom is evident in the ordered universe. Present from the beginning as God brings forth the created world, wisdom is perceived as having a part to play in God's creative activity (Prv chap. 8).

Akin to this theme is the personification of wisdom as a female who existed before all things were created and who reveals God in the world. Wisdom 7:25 says, "For she is an aura of the might of God / and a pure effusion of the glory of the Almighty; / therefore nought that is sullied enters into her." She is the street preacher who calls us to the divine banquet. She prepares the meal and invites those who seek wisdom to be seated at her table.

The theme most commonly addressed in the wisdom tradition is innocent suffering and the seeming randomness of life. The question of God's retribution for evildoing continues to plague us. We wonder if the evil events that transpire in our lives are the result of our own sinfulness or the sinfulness of our parents. We ask God why he has brought about suffering in our lives, or we accuse God by association when we ask why God has allowed suffering to take place. The story of Job wrestles with these questions. In Ecclesiastes, Qoheleth the preacher concludes that all is vanity and chasing after the wind (12:8).

Perhaps the most surprising thing that can be noted about the wisdom writings—particularly Job, Proverbs, and Ecclesiastes—is their secular nature. Unlike the Torah (Genesis through Deuteronomy), the Prophets, and the Historical Books, these books do not contain the themes common to Yahwism (the religion associated with the worship of Yahweh), nor do they recount the historical evolution of Israel's faith journey. Scholars have noted that these writings share common ideas with other ancient literature coming from Egypt and Mesopotamia. The wisdom of Israel was part of this broader movement that ultimately influenced the wisdom writings of the Bible.

Authorship of the Wisdom Literature

Who composed the wisdom books? The prophet Jeremiah offers some significant information for addressing this question when he mentions three important roles that existed in Israel during the time of his prophetic activity: "Come," they said, "let us contrive a plot against Jeremiah. It will not mean the loss of instruction from the priests, nor of counsel from the wise, nor of messages from the prophets" (Jer 18:18). The wise, known as sages, gave advice based on their observations and reflections. They collected ancient wisdom sayings and were responsible for the composition of the sapiential books. The term sapiential comes from the Latin sapiens, meaning "full of knowledge" or "discerning." Tradition attributed the writing of Proverbs, Ecclesiastes, and the Book of Wisdom to King Solomon, who is remembered for his great wisdom (1 Kgs 10:1–13).

It was not unusual to associate wisdom with the kings. In fact, attributing these books to Solomon was a common literary device intended to confirm the significance of the work and to invite readers carefully to consider the message. Attempts on the part of scholars to determine authorship of the wisdom writings have had limited results, as these works continued to develop over an extended time period.

The time frame for these writings spans the pre-exilic monarchial period (1000–587 BCE) and the post-exilic centuries (538–100 BCE). The majority of the wisdom writings are difficult to date. Only Sirach can be dated (180 BCE) with relative accuracy based on the foreword written by the author's grandson, who translated the work from Hebrew to Greek.

Literary Form and Content

The wisdom writings and the psalms are composed of several different literary forms, including poetry, hymns, proverbial sayings, poetic dialogues, blessings and curses, anecdotes, and dialectical material. Like shared wisdom today, ancient wisdom was passed on through the use of story, song, and wise sayings.

The Book of Job explores the question of innocent suffering. The story of Job's suffering and redemption frames a poetic debate that takes place between Job and his three friends, and Job and a young man named Elihu. Finally God appears to Job. The narrative establishes the context of the work as a kind of test called for by the accuser, named Satan, to see whether or not there is a person on earth who is righteous for righteousness' sake alone.

Proverbs consists of wise sayings and poetry presented by the king to his son. It is derived from observing life and intended to enhance the well-being of the king's son and all who read these words and take them to heart.

The author of Ecclesiastes, who refers to himself as Qoheleth, has failed to find meaning in life. His skeptical view pervades the work and raises questions about life's futility. In the end all that makes sense is fear of the Lord—that is, recognition that God alone holds the key to wisdom; everything else is chasing after the wind. Qoheleth's pessimism echoes human experience, for even today we can find ourselves struggling to make sense of life.

The author of Sirach (also called Ecclesiasticus, meaning "church book" from the Latin Vulgate) was Jesus, son of Eleazar, son of Sirach. He brings the wisdom tradition together with the history and piety of Israel. The author's grandson writes a preface for the book in which he explains that he has translated the work from its original Hebrew to Greek. He also sets out the purpose of Ben Sira's work, namely, ". . . to write something himself in the nature of instruction and wisdom, in order that those who love wisdom might, by acquainting themselves with what he too had written, make even greater progress in living in conformity with the divine law" (Sir foreword). In essence, Sirach brings wisdom into conversation with the Law and the Prophets.

The Wisdom of Solomon points to the wisdom and depth of Israel's faith and addresses the concerns of the Jewish faithful dispersed and living in a foreign culture. The instruction found in this book is addressed, not to the king's son as was typical, but to the leaders in the community who have status in governing the people.

The Song of Songs has a unique position in the wisdom tradition. Its placement in the canon was debated because it represented at its heart a love song. It is replete with effusive sexual metaphors and sings of the joys that the lovers find in each other. Its position in the canon means that it is understood to be an allegory of Yahweh's love for the people.

One book remains in our examination of the wisdom and poetry found in the Hebrew Bible, the Book of Psalms, also known as the Psalter. This work represents a collection of 150 songs of Israel, collected for prayer and worship in the second Temple. The psalms are arranged in five sections or books (Pss 1–41, 42–72, 73–89, 90–106, 107–150), each ending with a short doxology or a hymn of praise. The majority of psalms were composed by individuals and addressed to God. Some emerged out of the community, recalling the ways God was faithful to the Covenant made with Israel.

Modern scholars have identified types of psalms based on their literary forms and content. The major types are hymns of praise, individual and communal laments, thanksgiving, and wisdom psalms.

Scholars generally agree that Psalms 1, 32, 34, 37, 49, 112, and 128 are wisdom psalms. These psalms are not addressed to God but instead are didactic; that is, they provide instruction as a parent to a child. They employ wisdom forms of reflection and include typical wisdom themes.

Jews and Christians today continue to use the Psalter in prayer and worship. The Psalms were written by people who express their desires, their complaints, and their experiences as they implore God to answer their prayer. They are as relevant today as they were for the ancient Israelites. The words of the psalmist can speak for us in our struggles, "How long, Lord?" (Ps 13:1), and in our joys, "I praise you, so wonderfully you made me; / wonderful are your works!" (Ps 139:14).

Shannon Schrein, OSF, PhD
Professor and Chair
of Religious Studies
Lourdes College
Sylvania, Ohio

Introduction to the Prophets

Background

This section of the canon contains the materials of the literary prophets. The prophetic books are divided usually between the major prophets and the minor prophets, based on the length of the book, not on the importance of the message. Isaiah, Jeremiah, and Ezekiel are known as the major prophets, with the other twelve books making up the minor prophets, also known in Jewish terms as the "Book of the Twelve." In the Christian canon, the texts of Lamentations, Baruch, and Daniel also are found among the prophetic books, even though they do not technically fit within this category. Lamentations consists of a series of poems of lament upon the destruction of Jerusalem and the Temple by the Babylonians. Baruch contains writings attributed to the scribe of Jeremiah. Daniel is the only apocalyptic text in the Old Testament (see below).

The prophetic books cover a time period from the eighth century BCE to the fifth century BCE. These writings parallel the stories recorded in Samuel, Kings, Chronicles, Ezra, and Nehemiah. They provide a theological interpretation of the events that preceded the fall of Israel and Judah, the Exile, the return of the exiles to Jerusalem, life in Judea under the Persians and eventually the Greeks (Daniel). Amos and Hosea were prophets sent to speak to the northern kingdom of Israel. The other prophetic books are addressed either to the people of the southern kingdom (Judah), to the exiles in Babylon (and Egypt), or to those living in Judea.

Each book addresses a particular historical and cultural context, and therefore it must be interpreted first with consideration of what its messages were meant to say to the original audiences. However, these prophetic voices were preserved by the Jewish community for their enduring messages that spoke to Jews throughout the centuries. These messages spoke to the early followers of Jesus, and they continue to speak to the Church today.

Who Were the Prophets?

Understanding the definition of prophet is crucial to reading the prophetic books. The Hebrew prophets were not a unique phenomenon. Cultures surrounding Israel in the ancient Near East (e.g., Syria, Egypt, Mesopotamia, etc.) also had persons in their societies who fulfilled roles similar to those of the Hebrew prophets. The primary word used in Hebrew to identify a prophet is *navi*. The exact meaning of this word is hard to determine. It is thought to have Akkadian roots in a verb that means "to call, speak, or proclaim." From the examples found in the Old Testament, a prophet was someone called by God to speak on behalf of the divine to the people. Prophets were chosen by God to deliver a message for a particular time and to a specific group of people. The words that prophets spoke were not always what their audiences wanted to hear, but they were what the people needed to hear.

While the books of the Pentateuch identify Moses as a prophet, the official beginning of prophecy is dated to the ninth century BCE. Interestingly, the first person named as a prophet in the Bible is Moses' sister, Miriam (Ex 16:20). In the Talmud (Megillah 14a), the rabbis count forty-eight male prophets and seven female prophets in Israel; however, the Bible contains the names of only four women (Miriam, Deborah, Huldah, and Noadiah) who were prophets. The majority of the prophets are men, and all the prophetic books are named for males. The role of prophet emerged during the reign of David with the prophets Nathan and Gad, continuing through such dominant figures as Elijah and Elisha. In the eighth century BCE, a different kind of prophetic activity emerges as well as a new way to remember these personalities—through books that contain their messages as well as biographic and historical anecdotes. Whereas the early prophets tended to address primarily the leaders of the nation, the messages of the eighth-century prophets and their successors were directed at the whole community.

Despite popular opinion, the biblical prophets were not concerned with predicting the future as much as they were with giving a theological interpretation of the events taking place in the lives of the people. These divinely chosen messengers were covenant reminders who evaluated the behavior of the community based on the commandments provided to them by God through Moses. The cornerstone of these teachings were the Ten Commandments (Ex chap. 20, Dt chap. 5), which described both the vertical relationship (between God and humanity) and the horizontal relationships (among humans) that were required by God. It was the prophet's job to confront the people when they were not keeping covenant on either relational axis of the commandments. The prophets reminded the people that it was not enough to worship God if one was mistreating his or her neighbors, and vice versa. When the community failed to keep the commandments, the prophets saw the threat of outside forces as a consequence for their lack of covenant faithfulness. If the people did not re-establish a proper relationship with God, their fate at the hands of foreign enemies would be experienced as punishment from God. If, however, the people repented and returned to the Covenant, then, no matter what happened as a result of the actions of the Assyrians or Babylonians, the community would not have to doubt their relationship with God.

After the Assyrians and Babylonians wrought disaster on Israel and Judah, the prophets' messages turned to words of hope and restoration. Speaking to the exiles, the prophets provided assurance that God had not forgotten them and exhorted the community not to lose faith; restoration was coming. As the community became re-established in the land of Judea and covenantal requirements were again forgotten, the prophets once again reminded the people that they must remain faithful.

Apocalyptic and Prophetic Literature

Some time after the last prophetic book was composed, a new type of literature emerged in the Jewish community—apocalyptic literature. Though this style of writing shared some common elements with prophecy, it was not the same in tone and genre. Apocalyptic literature gets its name from the Greek word *apo kalypsis,* which means "revelation" or "uncovering." Daniel is the only true apocalyptic text in the Old Testament, but there are protoapocalyptic texts in Isaiah chapters 24 through 27. Ezekiel also contains some elements of this genre. Apocalyptic writing emerged during the Hellenistic period of Jewish history. In apocalyptic writing the author claims to have received a revelation about purported future events. The revelation is delivered through a heavenly messenger (i.e., an angel) to a human recipient. In Jewish apocalyptic literature, the alleged recipient was usually a well-known biblical character (e.g., Moses, Abraham, and so on). From the point of view of the authors, these future events were actually historical events. Like the prophets, writers of apocalyptic literature were addressing contemporary audiences about contemporary situations.

Times of persecution (political or religious) were the sociohistorical settings for apocalyptic writings. These texts were written to give encouragement to those enduring persecution by assuring them of God's salvation. Ultimately, good will triumph over evil. This truth often involved envisioning the judgment and punishment to be visited upon the oppressor. Typically, the materials were written using symbolic language in order to protect the writers from further persecution. This style of writing would have been familiar to an ancient audience, who would have known how to decipher the symbolism. Apocalyptic literature was written to reveal the near future and not to predict events that would not happen until millennia in the future. Like the prophetic literature, Daniel testifies to God's ultimate control and

to God's faithfulness in keeping covenant with Israel.

However, the majority of the prophetic literature is poetry, with prose materials used to provide narrative grounding for the oracles. The prose texts divide into autobiographical and biographical forms, including call narratives (stories of the prophets' divine call to their mission), vision reports (telling of divine revelations experienced by the prophets), reports of symbolic acts (actions taken by the prophets accompanied by an interpretation of their metaphorical message), and information about the events leading up to and surrounding the prophets' call. The poetic materials represent the bulk of the prophetic texts. Most of the messages delivered by the prophets are recorded as poetry and take the shape of prophecies of disaster and salvation, oracles, trial speeches, and disputation speeches.

Common Themes of the Prophets

Although the prophets were products of their time and culture, they all shared a common understanding of God and of Israel's role in the world. God is portrayed as the God of Israel and of the entire world. God is deeply concerned about humanity and expects people to act with concern for their neighbor more than for their own well-being. God is to be worshiped and demands the fidelity of God's People (i.e., no other gods). Israel is seen as God's Chosen People, who are called to live holy lives, marked by their difference from other cultures. Israel's chosen status is not an exclusive claim to God's love or a guarantee of special treatment. Rather, being chosen meant that Israel was called to live by a higher standard than other people and to be a light unto the nations. Everything the Israelites did was to reflect the kind of God they worshiped.

The prophets cared deeply about the people and saw themselves as connected to and revealing the emotions of the divine. Their anger was God's anger; their compassion was God's compassion. Their love and concern for Israel was what motivated them to say yes to God's call and to deliver God's words to the people. Prophets were optimists, despite their often negative portrayal of humanity. They believed that change or repentance was possible. They passionately proclaimed words of judgment in the hope that the people would see their wrongful ways and decide to return to a right relationship with God. Even though potential for change must have seemed highly unlikely at the time, if the prophets did not believe in the potential for change, their messages were in vain.

The opposite of this prophetic hope is seen in the Book of Jonah. In this fictional story, Jonah is portrayed as a prophet who did not want to prophesy for fear that the people would change. The great irony is that the story of Jonah is the only example of a prophet whose preaching was so powerful that his audience repented.

Even though the prophets of Israel were speaking to audiences more than two millennia ago and addressed specific historical situations, many of their messages are timeless. It is highly likely that one reason for preserving these prophetic works was the enduring value of their words. Faithfulness to God and God's demand for justice are ideas that are not bound by location or time. In every society, actions need to be taken to ensure the just treatment of all God's people, there are idols that compete for our worship, and there are those living in exile in need of hearing words of comfort and hope. Reading the prophets responsibly allows the community of faith to continue to benefit from their messages.

Lisa W. Davison, PhD
Professor of Old Testament
Lexington Theological Seminary
Lexington, Kentucky

· *The New Testament* ·

Introduction to the Gospels and the Acts of the Apostles

The Gospel and the Gospels

The word *gospel* appears in many places in the New Testament, but always in a singular, never in a plural form. For the earliest Christians, the word gospel (from the Greek *euangelion*) referred to the "good news" of what God had done in Jesus. The word gospel therefore is singular in all its seventy-six occurrences in the New Testament because it refers to this singular event and not to a written book as many contemporary readers might assume. It was not until the second century that Justin Martyr first used the plural form of the word to describe the narratives of Jesus' life and ministry that circulated among the early Christians. Properly speaking, each of the four narratives is an account of the one gospel, the "good news" about Jesus Christ, and only in a secondary sense are the written documents named "Gospels." The superscriptions "According to Matthew," "According to Mark," and so on, were added to manuscripts after the books themselves were in circulation.

Before we can engage in any serious study of the Gospels, we need to consider their literary genre. Although the other books in the New Testament adopted an already existing literary genre—usually a letter (e.g., Galatians), an epistle (e.g., James), or an apocalypse (Revelation)—many biblical scholars believe the Gospels are best understood as unique creations that embody a distinctly new literary genre. This new genre can best be described as a highly stylized and heavily symbolic theological narrative of historical events in the life of an individual—Jesus of Nazareth (though Luke's account of the Gospel also encompasses the life of the early Church in the Acts of the

Apostles). Yet other scholars contend that although these narratives are in many ways unique, they also strongly resemble Hellenistic biographies of the same period. Whether or not the Gospel genre is utterly original, the response these narratives seek to evoke is unique: faith in Jesus (Jn 20:31).

The Formation of the Gospel Accounts

Based on our brief description of the Gospel genre, the reader, or more precisely, the hearer of the Gospel accounts, did not think of these narratives simply as historical records. These texts certainly contain much historically reliable information about events in the life of Jesus and the early Church—a judgment widely accepted even by non-Christian scholars—yet the precise relationship of these books to the events they purport to narrate remains a point of disagreement. Some scholars argue that these books contain material created almost entirely by the early Church and thus bear little relationship to the events of Jesus' life. Other scholars believe that these books faithfully preserve the memory of what Jesus said and did even though material created by the early Church has also been inserted in places. Both groups of experts generally agree that some material in the Gospels comes from Jesus himself and some material reflects the concerns of the early Church. Distinguishing between these two types of material is part of New Testament study and is usually associated with what has come to be known as "historical Jesus research." Though some Christians find this area of study troubling, for Roman Catholics the distinction between the life and

ministry of Jesus and the proclamation of the early Church has been affirmed by the teaching office of the Catholic Church. Such a distinction, however, in no way detracts from the more fundamental conviction that the Gospels are true to the message, mission, and identity of Jesus.

Since the early twentieth century, biblical scholars have wrestled with how the Gospel tradition was formed. In 1964, the Pontifical Biblical Commission, then a teaching office of the Vatican, outlined the Roman Catholic Church's understanding of the development of the material in the Gospels (*Sancta Mater Ecclesia*). This account, reaffirmed at Vatican Council II in the *Dogmatic Constitution on Divine Revelation* (*Dei Verbum,* no. 19), states that the Gospels developed in three distinct yet interdependent stages. What follows is a summary of how New Testament scholarship generally views these three stages.

Stage I. The early followers of Jesus witness his proclamation of the nearness of God's Kingdom by word (pronouncements and parables) and action (symbolic actions and miraculous signs). Jesus' own role in the coming Kingdom is central. Jesus challenges the contemporary boundaries of Judaism, including prohibitions against table fellowship with known sinners and outcasts. He also calls into question the function of the Temple and confronts the religious and political establishment.

Stage II. The early followers of Jesus, almost all of whom had abandoned him at his hour of need, now proclaim him "Lord" and "Savior" in light of their experience of his Resurrection from the dead and the outpouring of the Spirit. Saul of Tarsus is converted to become a follower of Christ and embarks on a missionary career, leaving behind letters that he had written to various churches giving instructions on a wide variety of issues. Much of the apostolic preaching, or *kerygma,* contains little information about Jesus' life and ministry, though many remembrances of his pronouncements, miracles, and controversies are preserved in a variety of contexts by the early Christian Church.

Stage III. The proclamation of Jesus' saving work begins to take on a more narrative structure and gives way to the formation of the written Gospel accounts. These narratives incorporate material from both of the previous stages; however, they build a distinct portrait of Christ for the contemporary Christian Church.

These three stages illustrate the movement of the Gospel from the Apostles' experience of Jesus to an oral proclamation of the Good News, and then to a literary proclamation as well. This process or movement was accompanied by the development of a theology that sought to integrate more closely the life of Jesus with the proclamation of his Resurrection.

Upon reading the first three canonical narratives about Jesus, commonly called the Synoptic Gospels, the reader is struck by both the great number of verbal and structural similarities and by the uniqueness of many of the stories (the word *synoptic* means "seen together"). The precise nature and extent of the literary relationships among these texts has been an issue for centuries and is called "the synoptic problem." In the nineteenth century, the long-accepted priority of Matthew (i.e., that Matthew was the first Gospel composed and substan-

tially informed the Gospels of Mark and Luke) fell under suspicion, and Scripture scholars like K. Lachmann began to argue for the priority of Mark over Matthew and Luke. These scholars believed that Matthew and Luke started with the Gospel of Mark, which Matthew and Luke revised and to which they added material. This theory helped to explain the material common to all three synoptic accounts, yet there remained the problem of the two-hundred-twenty verses shared only by Luke and Matthew. In an effort to account for these verses, C. Weisse erected the so-called two-source hypothesis. He posited the existence of a collection of sayings from Jesus that circulated in the early church, and this source was eventually designated by the letter *Q,* an abbreviation for the German word *Quelle,* which means "source." According to the two-source hypothesis, Matthew and Luke had access to Q as well as Mark, when they composed their Gospels. Though some scholars are skeptical about the existence of Q, the two-source hypothesis is generally the preferred solution to the Synoptic Problem.

The Q source is not the only hypothetical source posited by New Testament scholars. There is much material in the New Testament, the origins of which are difficult to determine. The fourth Gospel (John) stands apart from the Synoptic Gospels as part of an early and unique tradition of Jesus' life and ministry, even though there are still some important points of contact with the *synoptics* (e.g., Jesus' cleansing of the Temple, walking on the sea, his entry into Jerusalem). This uniqueness has caused some to consider the material in John to be far removed from the life and ministry of Jesus, yet others (e.g., John Meier) have argued that some of the unique material in John may indeed go back to stage I. But virtually all scholars agree that the vast majority of the material in the Gospel of John reflects the unique theology and concerns of the late first-century Christian church. In addition to the Fourth Gospel, scholars struggle to account for special material in Matthew and Luke that is not related to Mark or Q (this material is often designated with the letters M and L). Like the Johannine material, the special Matthean and Lucan material reflects each of these authors' theological tendencies.

Christology in the Gospels

As one reads through the Scriptures, it is apparent that images of God and understandings of how God works in the world have developed over the course of time. For the earliest Christians, all of whom were Jewish, the experience of Jesus confirmed their prior experience of God but also challenged it. In the first century, Jewish men recited the Shema from Deuteronomy 6:4–9 (which begins "Hear, O Israel! The Lord is our God, the Lord alone!"). While the Shema was an affirmation of Israel's fidelity to Yahweh and not primarily a statement of monotheism, the prayer certainly illustrates that the declaration "Jesus is God" (i.e., Yahweh) would have been a difficult statement for early Jews. The fullest articulation of the Son's divinity, though powerfully implied in Jesus' own activity and broadly alluded to in the New Testament, awaited theological developments that did not take place until the fourth century (the Council of Nicaea). However, it is within the pages of the New

Testament that we begin to see the early Christians wrestle to find the precise language to articulate Jesus' relationship to God—a relationship made powerfully evident in the disciples' own experience of the Resurrection and the conversion it engendered within them. Their lives had been changed radically. They shifted from fleeing naked in the face of persecution (Mk 14:50–52) to offering bold witness in the face of death for the sake of Christ—to whom the earliest Christians "sang songs as to a god" (Pliny, *Letters,* 10.96).

As the earliest Christians struggled to find the language to express the relationship between Jesus and God, they employed and reinterpreted biblical imagery and vocabulary to express their convictions about Jesus. Some of this vocabulary took the form of christological titles (i.e., statements that were used to express faith in Jesus) or categories (i.e., a stock figure or image), including the following:

Lord. The Greek word *kyrios* has a wide range of meanings, from "sir" (Jn 4:11) to "Yahweh"—the name of God—in the Greek translation of the Hebrew Bible (the Septuagint). At the close of the Old Testament period, the divine name "Yahweh" was never pronounced (except by the high priest on the Day of Atonement). Instead the word Adonai (the Hebrew equivalent of "Lord") was pronounced. The title "Lord" was used to evoke the name of Israel's God, but it could function in other ways as well: (1) it was a way of referring to the glorified risen Christ, particularly with reference to Psalm 110:2; (2) it expressed the fact that this figure was due the same worship and honor as Yahweh (Phil 2:11); and (3) it expressed Jesus' dominion over all of Creation.

Messiah and Christ. The Aramaic word messiah simply means "anointed one"; it is translated into Greek as *christos.* It was customary in the ancient world to anoint people when they assumed important new positions in the community (i.e., king, priest, prophet). The title gradually became more associated with the king of Judah, though not exclusively. Following the Babylonian Exile (586–539 BCE), it began to be used in conjunction with Israel's hope of future restoration and deliverance, particularly the deliverance of Israel from Gentile oppression. Yet, it is clear from the New Testament itself that Jesus subverted the political expectations many had associated with the term messiah. It is perhaps the novelty, or the scandal, of calling the crucified Jesus Messiah that made it difficult for so many to respond to his disciples' proclamation of faith.

Son of God. In the Old Testament, the title "Son of God" is (1) a title given to angels (Jb 1:6); (2) a collective title for the people of Israel (Ex 4:22, Hos 11:1); and (3) a title of adoption for the king (Ps 2:7). The dominant view in the Old Testament is that a "Son of God" was someone who had received a God-given task. In the prologue of John's Gospel (Jn 1:1–18) and in John 3:16, Jesus is also called "the Father's only Son" (monogenes theos), emphasizing the uniqueness of his relationship with the Father and signaling a fuller understanding of Jesus' sonship as ontological—Jesus' very nature is the same as that of the Father. In Mark 1:11 the word son is used to translate the Hebrew word for "servant" and thus provides a link between "Son of God" and another popular category

for understanding Jesus, that is, that of "servant of God" in the Servant Songs found in Isaiah.

Son of Man. In Daniel 7:13, the "Son of Man" or "one like a Son of Man" (i.e., one who looks like a human being) is part of the heavenly court and helps to bring about the subjugation of the world and inaugurates the salvation of Israel (see also two Jewish apocalyptic works written around the time of Jesus, Enoch 46:1–4; 48:2–10; and 2 Esdras chap. 13). The phrase "Son of Man" appears to be Jesus' preferred self-designation because it is found in no early creedal formulae and only on his lips in the New Testament. Although this phrase is also used in Ezekiel when Yahweh addresses the prophet (3:17), in this context it simply differentiates the mortal prophet from the immortal and transcendent God (Yahweh) for whom he speaks.

These titles and categories, however, are not the only way the New Testament, and the Gospels in particular, express the religious significance of Jesus. The authors of the Gospels have selected specific narrative moments to express their convictions about Jesus. The late Raymond Brown called these literary scenes "christological moments." They are scenes taken from the life and ministry of Jesus that become the means by which New Testament authors give expression to their convictions about Jesus—convictions informed by the experience of the Resurrection. One of the clearest examples of a christological moment can be found in the opening chapters of two Gospel accounts—Matthew and Luke—where one finds two very different stories about the birth of Jesus.

While some basic details of these stories may have some root in stage I (see above), neither of these stories are historical accounts of Jesus' birth; rather, they offer portraits of Jesus as Davidic king (Matthew) and lowly, but universal, savior (Luke). Other examples of christological moments include the Virginal Conception, Jesus' Baptism, and the Transfiguration scenes. Each of these christological moments clearly and artfully points to the conviction of the early Church that in Jesus no less than God was present, bringing about the redemption of the world distorted by sin. Some readers may get mired in the question, "Did this event really happen?" However, the purpose of the Gospel accounts is to proclaim what God has done in Jesus.

The Acts of the Apostles and the Gospel Accounts

As mentioned above, the Gospel genre is somewhat indeterminate—like Hellenistic biographies but also quite different. No set boundaries exist for the proclamation of the Gospel that help account for the fact that one evangelist, Luke, has written a two-volume account. For Luke, the account of the Gospel includes the story of the early Christian community that is animated by the Holy Spirit. For Luke, it is the work of the Spirit that brings the Gospel to fruition in the life of the believing community. One would expect, therefore, that like the rest of Luke's Gospel account, the Acts of the Apostles contains important historical information on the early Church. But like his Gospel account, Luke's purpose in the Acts of the Apostles is not to provide merely a cold account of the facts; rather, in Acts, Luke proclaims the saving work

of God and creates a highly symbolic narrative to do so. This feature of Acts raises a question about the precise relationship between the historically reliable material in Acts and the creative activity of the evangelist; this question continues to leave modern scholars somewhat perplexed. In fact, if one compares the material in Acts to the material in Paul's letters, one finds many tensions and even discrepancies (e.g., Paul's account of his conversion and trip to Jerusalem in Galatians chapters 1 and 2 does not neatly correspond to Luke's narrative in Acts chapter 9). The question of Luke's source material for Acts remains intractable. In some instances Luke may have had written sources at his disposal (e.g., Acts 15:23–29 is thought by some to be the actual wording of a letter sent out to the churches from the so-called Council of Jerusalem). Additionally, there are places in the narrative of Acts where the narrator is inserted in the story—the so-called "we" sections of Acts. Some scholars have suggested that either the author was an eyewitness to the events narrated in these sections or perhaps the author of Acts used a written source, an itinerary or journal from an eyewitness. Thus, while the subject of Acts (i.e., the outpouring of the Holy Spirit and the growth of the Christian community) is distinct from the subject of the Gospel accounts (i.e., the life and ministry of Jesus), both nonetheless share a similar goal and a similar form, while at the same time raising similar historical issues.

Christopher McMahon, PhD
Assistant Professor of Theology
University of Mary
Bismarck, North Dakota

Introduction to the Letters and Revelation

The New Testament contains twenty-one books that bear the name "letter." In addition to these books, we find letters inserted into other documents of the New Testament, for example, the Acts of the Apostles and the Revelation to John. In other words, letters make up a substantial part of the New Testament. They were a commonly accepted form of communication in the ancient world, just as they are today. They also have a structure that is similar to today's letters. Therefore, ancient letters can be easier for modern readers to read and interpret than almost any other ancient literary genre. By contrast, the Book of Revelation is extremely difficult for modern readers to interpret correctly because the genre is not easily recognizable today.

The New Testament Letter Genre

The form or structure of New Testament letters or epistles is pretty predictable for the most part. First, they have an opening section that identifies the sender and the addressee, in that order, together with a greeting. Immediately following the opening, the letter usually includes a thanksgiving and a wish for the welfare of the addressee. Next is the body or main part of the letter, which contains the business or content of the letter. This section may also include exhortations to right behavior. The final part of the letter, the closing, usually contains greetings and good wishes for other people known to the addressee, along with a final greeting, wish, or prayer for the addressee.

How do the letters of the New Testament compare to other letters of the same time period? Many of the concerns that Paul writes about in his letters are typical of private letters of his time. Because they were originally intended for a single church or an individual, we have to remember that we are, in a sense, reading someone else's mail. Therefore, because we do not always know precisely what prompted his letter, we may not be able to fully understand Paul's correspondence. The letters addressed to churches were probably read at a time when the community was already gathered for worship, which may explain why Paul uses so much liturgical (i.e., worship-related) language in his letters.

What we have said about Paul's letters could be said of other letters in the New Testament, as well. However, some have only the appearance of a letter—perhaps an opening or closing greeting—but other parts of the book read more like a theological treatise or a homily. Although the author of these literary creations employs the form of the letter for rhetorical effect (to persuade and so on), most likely Paul never intended that they be sent as letters. The Letter to the Hebrews is a good example. Although it has a closing greeting and blessing like we might expect in a traditional letter (Heb 13:20–25), it has no opening address or thanksgiving section. The author uses first person pronouns ("we," "us") to address his audience in the second person ("you"), like one might expect in a letter, but much of the content is like a treatise in which he argues certain theological positions, while other parts are like a homily, exhorting the readers to stay faithful and not give up their faith in Jesus Christ.

The Organization of Paul's Letters

Although the New Testament includes thirteen letters that bear Paul's name, most biblical scholars agree that only seven were actually written by Paul. The others were most likely written by later disciples of Paul, who were either appealing to his authority or honoring his memory by attributing their letters to him. The letters attributed to Paul can be divided as follows:

- The authentic letters of Paul (also called Pauline Letters): These are 1 Thessalonians, 1 Corinthians, 2 Corinthians, Philippians, Philemon, Galatians, and Romans.

- The letters attributed to Paul but probably not actually written by Paul (also called Deutero-Pauline Letters): These are Ephesians, Colossians, and 2 Thessalonians.

- The Pastoral Letters, which are 1 Timothy, 2 Timothy, and Titus. The Pastoral Letters are so named because they are addressed to pastors or leaders of churches.

When you begin reading the letters attributed to Paul, you may wonder why they are arranged the way they are in the New Testament. As you might expect, we have no recorded history of the development of the New Testament manuscripts.

However, one thing we know for sure is that the order of the Pauline and Deutero-Pauline letters is not chronological. That is, the first one listed—the Letter to the Romans—is not the first one written. Instead, they appear to be organized from longest to shortest, with the letters addressed to churches first and the letters addressed to individuals second. The only exception is the Letter to the Galatians, which comes before the Letter to the Ephesians, even though the Letter to the Ephesians is slightly longer.

Thus, the canonical order of the letters attributed to Paul is as follows:

- The letters to churches (longest to shortest): Romans, 1 Corinthians, 2 Corinthians, Galatians, Ephesians, Philippians, Colossians, 1 Thessalonians, 2 Thessalonians

- The letters to individuals (longest to shortest): 1 Timothy, 2 Timothy, Titus, Philemon

The Organization of the Rest of the Letters

In addition to the thirteen letters attributed to Paul, the New Testament contains eight additional books bearing the title "letter." Like the letters attributed to Paul, they appear to have been arranged according to length, longest to shortest—Hebrews, James, 1 Peter, 2 Peter, 1 John, 2 John, 3 John, and Jude.

Except for the Letter to the Hebrews, which is relatively long, the other seven letters in this collection are rather short. Each of the seven is named for an Apostle or disciple of Jesus. However, today most biblical scholars think that all these letters are pseudonymous works (i.e., written by an anonymous author who was using the pseudonym of one of these famous persons). Some people today are troubled by the suggestion that the persons identified with these books did not actually write them, perhaps because it raises questions about the authority or reliability of the books. However, we should remember that ancient writers of sacred literature and their audiences were not as concerned about authorship as we are today. For them, the authority of these letters rested in the fact that they were somehow tied to the traditions of these famous religious figures, not that these people actually wrote the letters.

> **Some people today are troubled by the suggestion that the persons identified with these books did not actually write them, perhaps because it raises questions about the authority or reliability of the books.**

The seven letters attributed to the Apostles and disciples of Jesus are often grouped together and identified as the "Catholic Epistles." The word catholic means "general" or "universal." Some have understood this designation to mean that the letters were intended for a general audience, that is, they were not written for a particular individual church but for churches in a region or even for any church in general. Others have understood it to mean that this group of letters was universally accepted among the churches. Today many biblical scholars would question whether either of these explanations is appropriate. However, because these letters have been identified as such throughout the history of the Tradition, you will see that the designation "Catholic Epistles" continues to be used today.

The Book of Revelation and the Apocalyptic Genre

The English word apocalypse comes from a Greek word that means "revelation." Therefore, in some Bible translations, you will see the Book of Revelation referred to as "The Apocalypse," after its opening words. This title is appropriate because the book does contain revelations. John, the author of Revelation, describes his work as a record of the visions (images) and auditions (voices) that came to him through divine beings, usually angels. The subject matter of these visions and auditions are "heavenly things" and future events. However, John also describes his work as a prophecy, though he doesn't go so far as to call himself a prophet (1:3).

The term apocalyptic also describes a genre or type of literature that was relatively common from the second century BCE through the first century CE. Biblical scholars have suggested two possible sources for the apocalyptic genre. One is prophetic literature. In this regard, it is helpful to remember that the Old Testament prophets' messages were principally calls to conversion and divine consolation in times of trouble. Contrary to popular belief, the prophets did not, as a rule, engage in fortune-telling or what modern people understand as predicting the future. They did, however, rail against the people, saying that God would punish them if they continued in their wicked ways.

If apocalyptic literature in general and the Book of Revelation in particular have their roots in prophecy, this means that we should read these books as a call to conversion and a message of consolation written first for their original audiences living in their historical and cultural situation and now reinterpreted for our historical and cultural situation. Thus, today's believers should not be reading the Book of Revelation to find out what will happen in the end-time, but as a call to change our ways and renew our commitment to live the Gospel of Jesus Christ.

Other scholars argue that the apocalypse genre has its roots in wisdom literature. The Old Testament books included in this category are Job, Proverbs, and Ecclesiastes, along with the Book of Wisdom and Sirach (also known as Ecclesiasticus). Although wisdom literature covers a wide variety of topics, it is primarily concerned with questions about universal truth, the meaning of life (and death), and what constitutes human good. As one might expect, then, it also addresses issues of theodicy: Why do the righteous suffer while the wicked appear to go unpunished? What is the meaning of human suffering, and where is God's justice?

All of us can relate to these questions, especially when the difficulties of life become too much to bear. If apocalyptic literature and the Book of Revelation have their roots in the wisdom tradition, you can expect to see their authors assert the sovereignty and justice of God and express words of consolation to the suffering righteous. In the Book of Revelation we see these themes played out in John's numerous visions of the heavenly worship service, in which the four living creatures, the angels, and the martyred saints joyfully sing praises to God, who is all powerful and who rescues God's faithful ones from the forces of evil.

Catherine Cory, PhD
Associate Professor of Theology
University of Saint Thomas
Saint Paul, Minnesota

The Names of God in the Old Testament

The Judean theology flowered from its Semitic roots where El was a generic term for all the deities of Canaan. El and its derivatives later revealed Yahweh as El—the one true God.

Name	Significance	Reference
El (God)	A generic Semitic title for deity; the mighty powerful Creator; God of the Covenant; the protector	Gn 1:1,3,4,22; 17:7; 31:24; Is 44:24
Eloah; El Echad (the one God)	A generic name for deity; the one God who is savior, redeemer, and deliverer; the source of living water	Gn 45:5–6; Nm 23:22; Is 41:14; 43:3; 45:21; Jer 2:13; Mal 2:10
El Shaddai (God Almighty)	El Shaddai is a title of respect for the gods in the Canaanite pantheon; later became a name for Yahweh of Israel	Gn 17:1,7; 28:3; 35:11; 49:25; Ru 1:20–21; Ezr 1:2–4; 6:3; Ps 91:1; Is 9:6
El Rachum (God of compassion)	God, the compassionate one who suffers with the child in the womb (rechem in Hebrew means womb)	Dt 4:31; Neh 9:17
El Elyon (God most high)	Pre-Davidic God of Jerusalem; the faithful God; the most high	Gn 14:19–20; Nm 24:16; Dt 7:9; Ps 47:2–3
El Olam (God everlasting)	Eternal God of the universe; God of refuge and truth; originally a name for the Canaanite god of Beer-sheba but later became a name for Yahweh	Gn 21:33; Pss 31:5–6; 90:1–3; 93:2; 106:48; Is 26:4
El Yisrael; Hai; Elohe (God of Israel)	The living God; the Lord God of Israel; the holy one	Gn 33:20; Dt 5:26; 1 Sm 23:10; Ps 68:36; Is 5:16
El Gibbor (mighty God)	The God of war and strength; Lord; savior	Ex 15:2–3; Is 9:6
El Berith (God of the Covenant)	Pre-Israelite title for the Canaanite god of Shechem; later became a name for Yahweh	Jos 23:16; Jgs 9:46
Elohim (the single God)	Generic title for deity; signifies the singular, majestic God of Israel; plural form of El or Eloah—sons of heaven; can refer to Israel's God or to false gods	Gn 1:1,26; 6:2; 17:19; Ex 3:6; 20:3
Yahweh (life, existence, to be, Lord)	Personal name for God; I am who I am; the Creator; ruler of history; the deliverer; the tetragrammaton YHWH (pronounced Yahweh) was not spoken but was substituted with the word Adonai	Gn 4:26; 49:24–25; Ex 3:13–15; 2 Sm 22:2; Prv 9:10
Adonai (my great Lord)	Used as a substitute for Yahweh; also commonly used as a title of respect for a significant male, a lower lord, a social superior, a king, husband, father, or slave master	Ps 11:7; Jer 31:32; Hos 2:18; Mal 1:6
Yahweh Sabaoth (Lord of hosts)	Lord Almighty; conqueror and ruler of angels and deities; king of glory	Neh 9:6; Pss 24:10; 89:9–19; Is 1:24
Immanuel (Emmanuel); Yireh; El Roi (God with us)	A child who is a sign of God's presence; the one who sees all, hears the cries of his people, knows the affliction of slavery, and saves	Gn 16:13–14; 22:13–14; Dt 11:12; 2 Chr 16:9; 42:1; Jb 34:21–22; Is 7:10–17

Canons of Scripture
Old Testament (Hebrew Scriptures)

Jewish	Roman Catholic	Orthodox	Protestant
Torah (**Law**)	**Pentateuch**	**Pentateuch**	**Pentateuch**
Genesis	Genesis	Genesis	Genesis
Exodus	Exodus	Exodus	Exodus
Leviticus	Leviticus	Leviticus	Leviticus
Numbers	Numbers	Numbers	Numbers
Deuteronomy	Deuteronomy	Deuteronomy	Deuteronomy
Nevi'im (**Prophets**)	**Historical Books**	**Historical Books**	**Historical Books**
Early Prophets:	Joshua	Joshua	Joshua
Joshua	Judges	Judges	Judges
Judges	Ruth	Ruth	Ruth
1 and 2 Samuel	1 and 2 Samuel	1 and 2 Samuel	1 and 2 Samuel
1 and 2 Kings	1 and 2 Kings	1 and 2 Kings	1 and 2 Kings
Later Prophets:	1 and 2 Chronicles	1 and 2 Chronicles	1 and 2 Chronicles
Isaiah	Ezra	Ezra	Ezra
Jeremiah	Nehemiah	Nehemiah	Nehemiah
Ezekiel	*Tobit	*Tobit	Esther
Hosea	*Judith	*Judith	
Joel	Esther (*parts)	Esther (*parts)	
Amos	*1 and 2 Maccabees	*1, 2 and 3 Maccabees	
Obadiah		*4 Maccabees (as an	
Jonah		appendix)	
Micah		*1 and 2 Esdras	
Nahum	**Wisdom Books**	**Wisdom Books**	**Wisdom Books**
Habakkuk	Job	Job	Job
Zephaniah	Psalms	Psalms	Psalms
Haggai	Proverbs	Proverbs	Proverbs
Zechariah	Ecclesiastes	Ecclesiastes	Ecclesiastes
Malachi	Song of Solomon (Songs)	Song of Solomon	Song of Solomon
Kethuvim (**Writings**)	*Wisdom	*Wisdom	
Psalms	*Sirach (Ecclesiasticus)	*Sirach (Ecclesiasticus)	
Proverbs		*Prayer of Manasseh	
Job		*Psalm 151	
Song of Solomon			
Ruth	**Prophets**	**Prophets**	**Prophets**
Lamentations	Isaiah	Isaiah	Isaiah
Ecclesiastes	Jeremiah	Jeremiah	Jeremiah
Esther	Lamentations	Lamentations	Lamentations
Daniel	*Baruch	*Baruch	Ezekiel
Ezra	Ezekiel	Ezekiel	Daniel
Nehemiah	Daniel (*parts)	Daniel (*parts)	Hosea
1 and 2 Chronicles	Hosea	Hosea	Joel
	Joel	Joel	Amos
	Amos	Amos	Obadiah
	Obadiah	Obadiah	Jonah
	Jonah	Jonah	Micah
	Micah	Micah	Nahum
	Nahum	Nahum	Habakkuk
	Habakkuk	Habakkuk	Zephaniah
	Zephaniah	Zephaniah	Haggai
	Haggai	Haggai	Zechariah
	Zechariah	Zechariah	Malachi
	Malachi	Malachi	
35–39 Books	**46 Books**	**51 Books**	**39 Books**
(Some collections unite Samuel, Kings, and Chronicles.)	(♦Septuagint canon includes seven books not in the Hebrew canon.)	(Orthodox canon follows an expanded Septuagint canon that includes five or six additional books.)	(Protestant canon follows the Hebrew canon established in the first century CE.)

New Testament (Christian Scriptures)

Criteria for the Christian canon:
- written by an Apostle or the scribe of an Apostle
- agrees with the teachings and theology of the Apostolic Tradition
- widely known and used in the Christian community
- Roman Catholics, Orthodox, and Protestants all have the same twenty-seven books within the canon of the New Testament.

Roman Catholic	Orthodox	Protestant
Gospels	**Gospels**	**Gospels**
Matthew	Matthew	Matthew
Mark	Mark	Mark
Luke	Luke	Luke
John	John	John
Acts of the Apostles	**Acts of the Apostles**	**Acts of the Apostles**
Epistles (Letters)	**Epistles (Letters)**	**Epistles (Letters)**
Romans	Romans	Romans
1 Corinthians	1 Corinthians	1 Corinthians
2 Corinthians	2 Corinthians	2 Corinthians
Galatians	Galatians	Galatians
+Ephesians	+Ephesians	+Ephesians
+Colossians	+Colossians	+Colossians
Philippians	Philippians	Philippians
1 Thessalonians	1 Thessalonians	1 Thessalonians
+2 Thessalonians	+2 Thessalonians	+2 Thessalonians
+1 Timothy	+1 Timothy	+1 Timothy
+2 Timothy	+2 Timothy	+2 Timothy
+Titus	+Titus	+Titus
Philemon	Philemon	Philemon
Catholic Epistles	**Church Epistles**	**Church Epistles**
Hebrews	Hebrews	Hebrews
James	James	James
1 Peter	1 Peter	1 Peter
2 Peter	2 Peter	2 Peter
1 John	1 John	1 John
2 John	2 John	2 John
3 John	3 John	3 John
Jude	Jude	Jude
Apocalyptic	**Apocalyptic**	**Apocalyptic**
Revelation	Revelation	Revelation
27 Books	**27 Books**	**27 Books**

©2008 SAINT MARY'S PRESS

+Septuagint Canon
The Greek translation of the Hebrew Scriptures includes seven books [Deuterocanonical] not listed in the Hebrew or Protestant canons. The Septuagint [meaning seventy] was translated by the rabbis of Alexandria in 300–180 BCE. The Septuagint canon was affirmed at the Synods of Hippo [393 CE] and Carthage [397 CE] and adopted as the official list of Old Testament Books for the Roman Catholic canon at the Council of Trent in 1545 CE. Three hundred of the three hundred and fifty Old Testament references in the New Testament quote the Septuagint.

*Deuterocanonical Books
After the fall of Jerusalem to the Romans [70 CE], the Deuterocanonical works were removed from the Hebrew canon after the Jamnia Decision [100 CE]. The Roman Catholic canon includes the Deuterocanonical books and considers them inspired text. During the Reformation [1517–70 CE] the books were removed from the Protestant canon and considered apocrypha [false writings]. The Dead Sea scrolls, dating from 168 BCE–68 CE, include the Deuterocanonical books.

+Deutero-Pauline Epistles
Letters attributed to Paul but probably written by his followers.

The Historical Critical Method of Scripture Analysis

Christians hold that the Sacred Scriptures are the word of God, written in the words of human beings. Biblical scholars take numerous steps to study the Scriptures. The following represent the foundational approaches for scriptural research.

Method	Description and Analysis of the Text Used
Historical Criticism	Uncovers the historical situation (Sitz im Leben) of the world of the writer or editor. Examines the following: * the date and location of the writing community * the major social issues faced in a particular period * the cultural worldview of the writers or editors * the influence of the historical situation on the writing
Textual Criticism	Compares and contrasts various manuscripts of the Scriptures to determine the most authentic wording. Since the original manuscripts are no longer extant, textual criticism asks: * Which is the earliest surviving manuscript? * Which reading matches most of the available manuscripts? * What is the most likely reconstruction of the original text?
Form Criticism	Identifies the literary form and its function within the writing and the world of the writer. Asks the following: * Did the writer use a particular literary form, such as a poem, a historical story, a prophecy, a letter, a gospel? * Did the writer use a literary device such as a metaphor, an allegory, a midrash, a pun, a parable, or an exaggeration? * What was the cultural function of a particular literary form or device in the world of the writer?
Source Criticism	Identifies other writings known in the ancient cultures outside of the Scriptures that influenced the writer of a specific passage. Asks the following: * Did the writers build on an existing story or myth, or other literature as the basis for their work? * Does the theology or justice ethic of the biblical version vary from that of the cultural source?
Redaction Criticism	Analyzes the role and style of the editor who compiled various writings to produce the final version of a biblical work. Identifies the following: * unifying themes that the editor used to clarify teachings * particular symbols and wording used by the editor to teach biblical theology and ethics * the didactic intent of the editor

Sacred Time: Festivals, Feasts, and Fasts that Mark Biblical Events

Festivals include feasts to celebrate fertility, happiness, commitment, births, marriages, or victories. Times of fasting include penance and periods when feasting is forbidden.

Event	Significance and Reference
Sabbath	The seventh day is a day of rest to honor God and family. No work is permitted (Ex 20:8–11; Lv 23:1–3; Dt 5:12–15).
	Christians celebrate the Sabbath on Sunday to honor the Paschal mystery of Christ's life, death, and Resurrection (Mt 28:1–10; Mk 16:1–8; Lk 24:1–12; Jn 21:1–14).
Trumpets	New moon festival honors forty days of repentance and joy (Lv 23:23–25; Nm 28:11–15; Am 8:5).
New Year	Rosh Hashanah marks the New Year with prayers and rest. It anticipates the return of the Messiah and is a day of trumpets (Nm 29:1–6).
Yom Kippur or Day of Atonement	Ten days after the New Year, the Day of Awe marks the end of Trumpets and honors the ancestors. Repentance is symbolized by a scapegoat driven into the wilderness (Lv 16:29; 23:27; Nm 29:7–11).
	Christians associate the Day of Atonement with Jesus' sacrifice on the cross (Mt 26:28; Mk 14:24; Jn 8:12; Heb 9:11—10:18).
Sabbatical year	Every seven years the land rests, slaves are freed, and all debts are suspended or erased (Ex 21:2; 23:10–11; Lv 25:1–7; Dt 15:1–6).
Jubilee (fiftieth year)	The seventh sabbatical year is honored with compassion to the poor, the freedom of slaves, erasure of debts, the return of property to its original owner, and resting the land (Lv 25:8–22; 2 Chr 36:21; Is 61:1–2).
Pilgrimage festivals	The feasts of Passover, Unleavened Bread, Weeks, Booths (or Tabernacles), and the harvest were marked with pilgrimages to the sanctuary or Temple in Jerusalem (Ex 23:14–17; 34:22–23; Dt 16:16–17).
Feast of Passover or Unleavened Bread	The memorial of the Exodus from Egypt is honored in a seder meal in which prayers and blessings are offered for Jews across the world (Ex 12:1–28; 34:18,25; Lv 23:4–14; Nm 9:1–14; 28:16–25; Dt 16:1–8; Ez 45:18–24).
	Jesus memorialized Passover as he offered himself as the bread of life (or the Eucharist) (Mt 26:17–19,26–29; 1 Cor 10:1; 11:23–26; Eph 2:19–20).
Feast of Weeks	The seven weeks of harvest after the blessing of the first sheaf of barley in the rite of Omer during Pentecost (Ex 23:16; 34:22; Lv 23:15; Nm 28:26–31; Dt 16:9–10).
Pentecost	Pentecost concludes seven weeks after the rite of Omer as the first sheaf of grain is offered in thanks for the harvest. The feast of Weeks or Shavuot marks fifty days after Passover (Lv 23:15–22; Nm 28:26–31).
	Pentecost, for Christians, marks the descent of the Holy Spirit and reveals Christ's Church (Acts 2:1–11; 20:16; 1 Cor 16:8).
Feast of Tabernacles or Booths	Autumn feast; gathering of the harvest on the fifteenth to the twenty-first days of the seventh month. The ingathering of the harvest marks Sukkoth, when Israel lived in the wilderness (Lv 23:33–43; Nm 29:12–39; Dt 16:13–17; Ez 45:25; Zec 14:16–19).
	The Transfiguration of Jesus took place at the feast of Tabernacles (feast of Booths) (Lk 9:33; Jn 7:2,37).
Feast of Shiloh	A version of Tabernacles or Booths during which families made pilgrimages to Shiloh (Jgs 21:19; 1 Sm 1:1–7).
Purim	Holy day that marks the defeat of Haman of Persia by Esther and honors Mordecai's faith. The feast includes drama, fasting, feasting, and prayers for Israel (Est 9:20–32).
Hanukkah	The dedication of the second Temple and the defeat of Antiochus IV (167 BCE) by the Maccabean Wars is the mythic source of Hanukkah. The festival includes gift giving, feasting, and celebrations (1 Mc 4:1–59; 2 Mc 10:1–8; Jn 10:22).

Numbers and Their Significance in the Bible

The ancient biblical languages of Hebrew and Aramaic could communicate meaning both phonetically and numerically. Certain letters had a numerical value and symbolic significance. The writers of the Scriptures used numbers to address significant values or to assert a reversal or a lack of value.

Number and Meaning	Significance and Reference
Three Completeness; balance	Three-year-old animals were used for sacrifice (Gn 15:9). Prayers were offered at dusk, dawn, and noon (Ps 55:17–18; Dn 6:11). Jonah spent three days and nights in the belly of a fish (Jon 2:1). The Son of Man rises on the third day (Mt 20:19).
Four, Forty Balanced forces for healing or a new creation (e.g., it takes forty weeks of pregnancy to birth a child)	Eden birthed four rivers—Pishon, Gihon, Tigris, and Euphrates (Gn 2:10–14). The deluge raged for forty days and forty nights (Gn 7:12). The Israelites wandered for forty years in the desert (Nm 32:13). Forty thousand troops fought the battle of Jericho (Jos 4:13). David and Solomon reigned for forty years (2 Sm 5:4; 2 Chr 9:30). The four corners of the earth mark the four directions (Is 11:12; Rv 7:1). Four living creatures stand before God (Ez 1:10; Rv 4:6–8). Nineveh was warned for forty days (Jon 3:4). Jesus fasted in the desert forty days and forty nights (Mt 4:2). The resurrected Christ appeared for forty days (Acts 1:3). On the fortieth day Christ ascended into heaven (Acts 1:9–11). Moses hid in the desert for forty years (Acts 7:29–30).
Six Ominous and mysterious, the number six warns of danger or shame. It anticipates change and new birth in the coming of the seventh.	God created all that is in six days. Six days are for work (Gn 1:31; Ex 16:26). In Exodus, Pharaoh sent six hundred chariots to defeat Israel (Ex 14:6–8). Sinai was covered with the cloud for six days (Ex 24:16). Purification after giving birth to a girl requires sixty-six days (Lv 12:5). Joshua circled Jericho for six days (Jos 6:3,14). Daniel was in the lions' den for six days (Dn 14:31). In the sixth month the angel Gabriel came to Mary (Lk 1:26). At Cana Jesus turned six stone jars of water into wine (Jn 2:6). Mary of Bethany anointed Jesus six days before Passover (Jn 12:1). The number of the beast is 666 (Rv 13:18).
Seven Perfection, totality, the infinite, or its opposite. Multiples of seven (forty-nine, seventy, seventy-seven, and 144,000) carry similar symbology.	Sabbath is the seventh day (Gn 2:2–4). The seventh year equates freedom. The forty-ninth year is Jubilee (Ex 21:2; Lv 25:8–10). Seventy elders beheld visions of God (Ex 24:1,9). Pentecost is seven weeks after Passover (Lv 23:15–16; Acts 2:1–6). Solomon built the Temple in seven years (1 Kgs 6:37–38). God preserved a remnant of seven thousand faithful Israelites (1 Kgs 19:18). There are seven gifts of the Spirit (Is 11:1–2). The Exile lasted for seventy years (Jer 25:11–12). Jesus blessed seven loaves and had seven full baskets left (Mt 15:34,37). Jesus taught us to forgive seven times and seven times seventy times (Mt 18:21–22). Jesus healed Mary Magdalene of seven demons (Mk 16:9). Visions of Christ include several references to the number seven (Rv 1:17–20).
Nine As a multiple of three, nine symbolizes life (e.g., it takes nine months for a baby to develop in the womb).	Elders live to be nine hundred years old as a symbol of wisdom (Gn 5:5). Abraham received God's Covenant when he was ninety-nine years old (Gn 17:1). Defeat of nine hundred chariots required divine intervention (Jgs 4:3,13). The Crucifixion was at the ninth hour (Mk 15:25).
Twelve (four threes) Wholeness, the life force, and completion	Ishmael is the father of twelve chieftains (Gn 17:20). Moses set up twelve pillars for the twelve Tribes of Israel (Ex 24:4). Isaac is patriarch of twelve Tribes (Ez 47:13). Jesus healed a woman of a twelve-year hemorrhage (Mt 9:20–22). Jesus chose twelve Apostles (Mk 3:14–19). Jesus astounded the teachers of the Law at the age of twelve (Lk 2:41–42). New Jerusalem has twelve gates, twelve guardian angels, and twelve stone foundations (Rv 21:10–14). The tree of life bears fruit twelve times a year (Rv 22:2).

Deities of the Greco-Roman Empire

The Romans loved everything Greek, including their numerous gods. Many gods shared both Greek and Roman names. Some were benign, but others were violent and lustful. The Christians rejected them as demons and their erotic murderous rites as sorcery [1 Cor 10:20-21; Rv 9:20-21]. The New Testament embraces the God of the Jews as the one Creator and Jesus as the sole Lord.

Name	Significance and Reference
Greek: Zeus Roman: Jupiter	Olympian father of the gods noted for his insatiable lust imposed on divinities and mortals. Antiochus erected his statue in the Jerusalem Temple and honored him on Mount Gerizim as Zeus the Hospitable. Athenian Greeks thought Paul's companion, Barnabas, was the incarnation of Zeus (2 Mc 6:1–5; Acts 14:12–13).
Greek: Apollo Roman: Apollo	Olympian son of Zeus and twin of Artemis, Apollo is imaged as the god of culture, art, poetry, civilization, and harmony.
Greek: Artemis Roman: Diana	Olympian great mother of the Ephesians and the virgin sister of Apollo, Artemis is the goddess of the hunt and protector of children (Acts 19:24–35).
Greek: Ares Roman: Mars	Olympian god of war, bloodshed, and eroticism. Paul gave his speech about the unknown god while standing on the Areopagus (Hill of Ares) near the Athenian acropolis (Acts 17:22–26).
Greek: Hermes Roman: Mercury	Olympian messenger; son of Zeus; god of merchants. The Greeks thought Paul was Hermes (Acts 14:12–13).
Greek: Hades	Known as the god of the underworld (Sheol in Hebrew) or the netherworld of the dead, Hades became a title for the fires of hell (Mt 11:23).
Greek: Attis	Known as the god of fertility, Attis was revered, along with his consort Cybele, by devotees who castrated themselves.
Greek: Rhea Roman: Rhea East: Cybele	Known in Asia Minor as the mother of the gods, Rhea was honored across the Roman Empire, along with her consort Attis, in frenzied, erotic rites that included self-mutilation.
Greek: Aphrodite Roman: Venus	This Olympian Greek goddess of sex, love, and beauty was known as the heavenly one born from sea foam. Christians condemned Aphrodite's orgiastic rites. Her title "morning star" was mocked and polemically given to Jesus. Her image is a blend of the Canaanite Astarte and the Assyrian Ishtar. Cupid is her messenger, Adonis her son and lover (Jude 13; 2 Pt 1:19–21; Rv 22:16).
Greek: Athena Roman: Minerva	Olympian daughter of Zeus and goddess of wisdom, Athena is the patron of Athens and of war. The Parthenon (the Temple of the Maiden) was dedicated to Athena.
Greek: Asclepius (Asklepios) Roman: Aesculapius	Greek god of healing and medicine. Nephew of Artemis and son of Apollo and the mortal Coronis, he is an astral god seen in the constellation Ophiuchus (the Serpent Bearer). His symbol is a staff entwined with serpents—the caduceus of the medical profession. Miracle healing stories of Jesus diminished the power of Asclepius for Greek converts to Christ.
Greek: Dionysus Roman: Bacchus (Liber)	Son of Zeus and Semele, he is known as the god of wine, the theatre, and eroticism. His rites included cannibalism. Devotees wore wreaths of ivy. Under Antiochus, Jews were forced by penalty of death to wear ivy and march in processions for Dionysus (2 Mc 6:7–10; 14:33).
Greek: Mithras Roman: Mithras	A blend of Persian astral deities, he has been imaged as Taurus, Scorpio, the serpent Hydra, Canis Minor the dog, and the raven Corvus. The savior god of the Roman mystery cult, he was worshiped in subterranean chambers. Constantine was a devotee before his conversion.
Egyptian: Isis	A fertility goddess, her cult thrived until 300 CE. In Rome she was a manifestation of all goddesses: Cybele, Minerva, Venus, Juno, Proserpina, Ceres, Diana, Gaia, Rhea, Bellona, Hecate, and the moon.
Emperor worship	Alexander the Great, Nero, Caligula, and Domitian deified themselves and forced the populace to honor them as gods. Condemnations of this idolatry are noted in apocalyptic imagery (Mt 24:15; Mk 13:14; Rv 14:11; 20:4).

Deities of the Ancient Middle East

The writers of the Scriptures taught strict monotheism and equated idolatry with injustice, adultery, sorcery, and harlotry. Some gods and goddesses were benign, but others demanded human sacrifice, infanticide, and murder. The image of God in the Scriptures is in direct contrast with the nature, demands, and rites of the idols of the ancient Middle East.

Name	Significance	Reference
Strange gods; gods of the nations	Idolatry refers to worship of foreign deities; the use of graven images, sex rites, human sacrifice, and cannibalism; and betrayal of the Lord God.	Dt 31:16; Jgs 2:12; 1 Chr 16:26; 2 Chr 33:6–7; Wis 12:4–7
El (sky god)	The Canaanite high god, a generic word for deity. El became the title for Lord God and was used in place and personal names.	Gn 32:29; 33:20; Jos 19:38; Jgs 9:46; Ps 69:7
Baal	A Canaanite word that referred to many deities. Baal was a fertility thunder god and was worshiped with Asherah or Anath. The title Baal meant lord, master, or named a place.	Jgs 2:13; 1 Kgs 16:32; 2 Kgs 5:18; 17:31; Jer 19:5; Hos 2:15,18
Leviathan	Deity of the sea, a dragon or serpent, the enemy of God. Leviathan evolved from the Semitic serpent Tiamat—imaged as waters of chaos, or the abyss. Also known as Rahab, the dragon. Egypt, Assyria, and Babylon were symbolized as the serpent of chaos.	Jb 9:13; 26:12; 40:25–32; Pss 74:14; 89:11; Is 27:1; 51:9
Molech	Canaanite death god whose child sacrifice rites were performed on the high places. The rites of Molech blended with rites of Chemosh of Moab and Milcom of the Ammonites.	1 Kgs 11:5–9,33; 2 Kgs 23:10–13; 2 Chr 28:3; Jer 7:31; 32:35; Acts 7:43
Asherah (Anath)	In Canaan, the goddesses of the Middle East were known collectively as Asherah. Asherah was worshiped as Anath, the consort of Baal-Hadad, and as Ashima. Her symbol was a tree, pillar, or pole—also called an asherah.	1 Kgs 14:23; 16:32; 18:19; 2 Kgs 17:29–31
Astarte	The goddess of storms, Astarte's rites were practiced on the Mount of Misconduct. She was called Asherah and the horror of Sidon and of Moab.	1 Sm 31:10; 1 Kgs 11:5–9,33; 2 Kgs 23:13–15
Ishtar of Babylon (Inanna of Sumer)	Assyrian deity of sex, war, and fertility imaged as the serpent of Eden whose fruit was death. In Israel, Ishtar was blended with the queen of heaven and Astarte. Her sacred tree connected her to Asherah. Over time the serpent came to symbolize sin and death.	Gn 3:3–4; Sir 21:2; Jer 7:18; 44:17–19; Ez 8:14
Tammuz (Dumuzi of Sumer)	Babylonian god of vegetation, the consort and son of Astarte (Ishtar) for whom seasonal weeping rituals were performed.	Ez 8:14
Dagon	Fierce fertility god of ancient Mesopatamia adopted by the Philistines, Dagon was the god of corn, beans, grain, and the underworld. Like Chemosh, he was imaged as a fish. His temples were in Beth-shan, Ashdod, and Gaza.	Jgs 16:23; 1 Sm 5:1–5,7; 1 Chr 10:10; 1 Mc 10:83–84; Jon 2:1
Hosts of Heaven (Zodiac)	Star gods of Babylon revered by divination and astrology demoted to the status of creations of Yahweh, the God of hosts. Worship of the queen of heaven was connected to this practice.	Dt 4:19; 2 Kgs 21:1–5; Neh 9:6; Sir 17:27; Jer 8:2; 44:25
Bel Marduk	Chaldean war and thunder deity. In Babylon, Bel was known as Merodach. In Exile, the Judeans were forced to perform the rites of the serpent Ishtar and Bel Marduk. Talismans of Bel were hung on animals.	Is 46:1; Jer 50:2

Colors and Their Significance in the Bible

Colors were precious in the ancient world. The most treasured were scarlet, crimson, purple, and blue. The Egyptians made a dye from a shellfish called *Carthamus tinctorius*. The Hebrews and Phoenicians created the stain from the shellfish *chelzon* and the dried skeleton of the *Coccus ilicis*, a worm that protected its eggs by attaching itself to oak trees called *kermes* in Arabia. The colors came to symbolize wealth, power, and election.

Color	Significance and Reference
Crimson	A crimson thread was a sign of election of the firstborn (Gn 38:28).
	Solomon included crimson in the decor of the Temple (2 Chr 2:6).
	A crimson veil honored the Temple, its rite and sacrifice (2 Chr 3:14; Heb 9:19).
	Crimson was a sign of wealth and power (Jdt 10:21).
	Revered as treasure (1 Mc 4:23)
	Sign of greed and injustice, the stain of sin (Is 1:18)
	A sign of blood, evidence of deadly victory in war (Na 2:4)
Scarlet	Scarlet was a sign of the blood of sacrifice; listed with ritual elements and liturgical vestments (Ex 25:3–7; 26:36; Lv 14:6).
	The high priest's ephod, girdle, and breastplate had scarlet on them (Ex 28:6–15).
	A scarlet cord was the sign of protection for Rahab's family (Jos 2:18).
	Symbol of wealth, prosperity, and beauty (2 Sm 1:24; Song 4:3)
	Scarlet was a sign of divine favor and care (Sir 45:1,11).
	Roman soldiers mocked Jesus with royal scarlet (Mt 27:28; Lk 23:11).
Red	Esau, the red skinned, sold his birthright for red lentils (Gn 25:25–34).
	Color of blood and of the red heifer of sacrifice (Nm 19:2; 2 Kgs 3:22)
	Color of perfected wine and health (Prv 23:31; Song 5:10)
	The red horse was a sign of angelic guardians, the four winds, or violence (Zec 1:8–11; 6:2–4; Rv 6:4).
Vermilion	A vivid red toxic paint made from the mineral cinnabar. This mercuric sulfide was a sign of harlotry and idolatry (Ezr 23:14).
	The prophets cited a vermilion painted house as a sign of opulence and allegiance with injustice (Jer 22:14).
Purple	Purple draped altars were a sign of God's presence (Nm 4:13).
	Purple is a sign of beauty and culture; a sign of kings and a display of grandeur; a sign of opulence and greed (Jgs 8:26; Est 8:15; 1 Mc 8:14; Jer 4:30).
	Phoenician artisans were known for their purples (2 Chr 2:13; Song 3:10).
	Wisdom was symbolized as a purple cord (Sir 6:30).
	Colors of heaven, prayer, wealth, and prestige (Ez 27:7; Lk 16:19)
	Jesus was mocked by Roman soldiers with a purple cloak (Mk 15:17; Jn 19:2).
	Lydia, the first baptized European, was a seller of purple (Acts 16:14).
	Purple became the sign of the harlot and those who place their faith in wealth (Rv 17:4; 18:12–17).
Blue or Violet	Woven into the veil and curtain of the holy of holies (Ex 26:31–36)
	Bezalel of Judah embroidered and wove colored cloth (Ex 38:22–23).
	Blue (and violet) was woven into tassels, garments, and prayer shawls as a sign of the Law and of Israel as children of God (Ex 39:8; Nm 15:37–41).
	Blue was a sign of idolatrous worship and injustice (Bar 6:11).
	Blue was worn by the warriors of Assyria (Ez 23:5–6).
	Heavenly color of prayer; a sign of angelic warriors (Rv 9:17)
	Blue sapphires were set in the heavenly walls of Jerusalem (Rv 21:19–20).
White	Healthy teeth and bone were compared to white milk. Manna was white and forgiveness made sin white as snow (Gn 49:12; Ex 16:31; Is 1:18).
	White was worn by angels and was a sign of the Holy One (2 Mc 11:8; Mt 17:2).
	White represented fine clothing (Eccl 9:8).
	Color of purity, awe, light, and dazzling response (Is 1:18; Jn 20:12)
	A white horse was a sign of victory (Zec 6:3; Rv 2).
Black	Black was the color of healthy hair, skin free from leprosy (Lv 13:31).
	Black was the color of a storm and the darkness of night (1 Kgs 18:45; Jer 4:28).
	Black could symbolize devastation; mourning (Jb 30:30).
	Black was a sign of beauty (Song 1:5; 5:11).
	A sign of heavenly winds or divine judgment (Zec 6:2; Rv 6:5,12)

Expanded Timeline of Biblical History

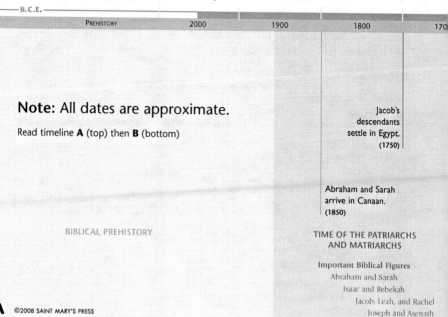

PREHISTORY | 2000 | 1900 | 1800 | 170

Note: All dates are approximate.

Read timeline **A** (top) then **B** (bottom)

Jacob's descendants settle in Egypt. **(1750)**

Abraham and Sarah arrive in Canaan. **(1850)**

BIBLICAL PREHISTORY

TIME OF THE PATRIARCHS AND MATRIARCHS

Important Biblical Figures
Abraham and Sarah
Isaac and Rebekah
Jacob, Leah, and Rachel
Joseph and Asenath

A   ©2008 SAINT MARY'S PRESS

Expanded Timeline of Biblical History
PROPHETS

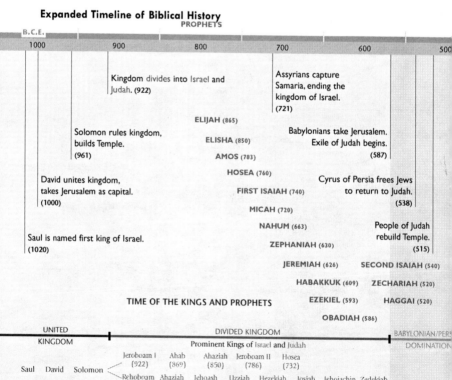

B.C.E.

1000 | 900 | 800 | 700 | 600 | 500

Kingdom divides into Israel and Judah. **(922)**

Assyrians capture Samaria, ending the kingdom of Israel. **(721)**

ELIJAH (865)

Solomon rules kingdom, builds Temple. **(961)**

ELISHA (850)

Babylonians take Jerusalem. Exile of Judah begins. **(587)**

AMOS (783)

HOSEA (760)

David unites kingdom, takes Jerusalem as capital. **(1000)**

FIRST ISAIAH (740)

Cyrus of Persia frees Jews to return to Judah. **(538)**

MICAH (720)

NAHUM (663)

People of Judah rebuild Temple. **(515)**

Saul is named first king of Israel. **(1020)**

ZEPHANIAH (630)

JEREMIAH (626)   **SECOND ISAIAH (540)**

HABAKKUK (609)   **ZECHARIAH (520)**

TIME OF THE KINGS AND PROPHETS

EZEKIEL (593)   **HAGGAI (520)**

OBADIAH (586)

| UNITED KINGDOM | DIVIDED KINGDOM | BABYLONIAN/PERS DOMINATION |

Prominent Kings of Israel and Judah

| | Jeroboam I (922) | Ahab (869) | Ahaziah (850) | Jeroboam II (786) | Hosea (732) | | | |
| Saul | David | Solomon | Rehoboam (922) | Ahaziah (842) | Jehoash (837) | Uzziah (783) | Hezekiah (715) | Josiah (640) | Jehoiachin (598) | Zedekiah (597) |

B   ©2008 SAINT MARY'S PRESS

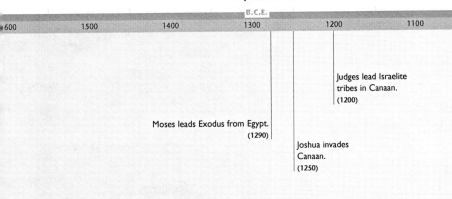

Expanded Timeline of Biblical History

B.C.E.

| 1600 | 1500 | 1400 | 1300 | 1200 | 1100 |

Judges lead Israelite
tribes in Canaan.
(1200)

Moses leads Exodus from Egypt.
(1290)

Joshua invades
Canaan.
(1250)

TIME IN EGYPT AND THE EXODUS

Important Biblical Figures
Moses
Aaron
Miriam

TIME OF THE JUDGES

Important Biblical Figures
Deborah
Gideon
Samson
Samuel

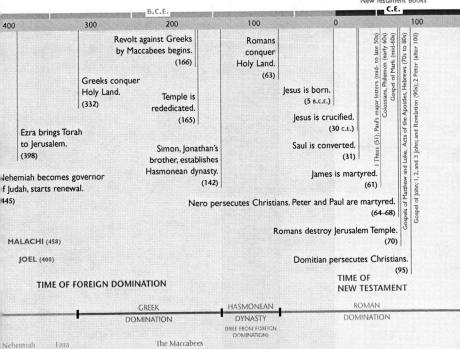

Expanded Timeline of Biblical History

New Testament Books

B.C.E. **C.E.**

| 400 | 300 | 200 | 100 | 0 | 100 |

Revolt against Greeks
by Maccabees begins.
(166)

Romans
conquer
Holy Land.
(63)

Greeks conquer
Holy Land.
(332)

Temple is
rededicated.
(165)

Jesus is born.
(5 B.C.E.)

Ezra brings Torah
to Jerusalem.
(398)

Jesus is crucified.
(30 C.E.)

Simon, Jonathan's
brother, establishes
Hasmonean dynasty.
(142)

Saul is converted.
(31)

Nehemiah becomes governor
of Judah, starts renewal.
(445)

James is martyred.
(61)

Nero persecutes Christians. Peter and Paul are martyred.
(64–68)

MALACHI (458)

Romans destroy Jerusalem Temple.
(70)

JOEL (400)

Domitian persecutes Christians.
(95)

1 Thess (51); Paul's major letters (mid- to late 50s)
Colossians, Philemon (early 60s)
Gospel of Mark (mid-60s)
Gospels of Matthew and Luke, Acts of the Apostles, Hebrews (70s to 80s)
Gospel of John; 1, 2, and 3 John; and Revelation (90s); 2 Peter (after 100)

TIME OF FOREIGN DOMINATION

**TIME OF
NEW TESTAMENT**

| GREEK
DOMINATION | HASMONEAN
DYNASTY
(FREE FROM FOREIGN
DOMINATION) | ROMAN
DOMINATION |

Nehemiah   Ezra   The Maccabees

THE KINGDOM YEARS

Probable extent of Israelite control during the Kingdom of Solomon, c. 950 B.C.

The Kingdoms of Israel and Judah, c. 860 B.C.

---- Boundary between Israel and Judah

? Exact location questionable

0   75 miles

0   75 kilometers

Riblah

Zobah

Byblos

+ MT. LEBANON

Sidon

Phoenicia

Damascus

*The Great Sea
(Mediterranean Sea)*

Tyre

+ MT. HERMON

Dan

ARAM
(Syria)

Kedesh

Hazor

Acco

Sea of
Chinnereth

Ashtaroth

Golan?

+ MT. CARMEL

Jokneam

River Yarmuk

Dor

Megiddo

Jezreel

Ramoth Gilead

Taanach

MT. GILBOA

Dothan

Jabesh Gilead

Tirzah

Zaphon

Samaria

Succoth

Shechem

River Jordan

Aphek

Shiloh

ISRAEL

Joppa

Northern Kingdom

Bethel

Ammon

Gezer

Mizpah

Heshbon

Philistia

Jerusalem

Azekah

Bethlehem

Medeba

Ashkelon

Adullam

Tekoa

Dibon

Gaza

Eglon?

Debir

Hebron

River

Aroer

Ziklag?

Dead
Sea
(Salt
Sea)

Arnon

Arad

Beersheba

Moab

Kir Hareseth

Zoar

Brook Zered

JUDAH
Southern Kingdom

Bozrah

Kadesh Barnea

Edom

Brook of Egypt

Teman

© 2001 by Thomas Nelson, Inc.
and Saint Mary's Press

Ezion Geber

Elath

maps.com

76

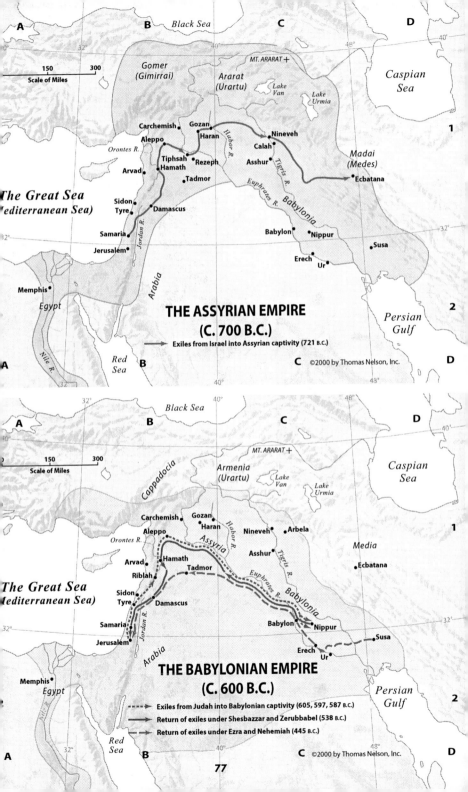

THE ASSYRIAN EMPIRE
(C. 700 B.C.)

→ Exiles from Israel into Assyrian captivity (721 B.C.)

©2000 by Thomas Nelson, Inc.

THE BABYLONIAN EMPIRE
(C. 600 B.C.)

••••➤ Exiles from Judah into Babylonian captivity (605, 597, 587 B.C.)

——➤ Return of exiles under Shesbazzar and Zerubbabel (538 B.C.)

— —➤ Return of exiles under Ezra and Nehemiah (445 B.C.)

©2000 by Thomas Nelson, Inc.

77

THE MINISTRY OF JESUS

(1,742) Elevation, in feet

? Exact location questionable

0 ——— 30 miles
0 ——— 30 kilometers

Sidon

Damascus

Zarephath

MT. LEBANON
(11,000)

MT. HERMON
(9,200)

Iturea

Tyre

Phoenicia

Panias
(Caesarea Philippi)

Trachonitis

Galilee

Ptolemais

Chorazin

Bethsaida?

Capernaum

MT. CARMEL
(1,742)

Cana

Magdala

Sea of
Galilee

Gergesa

River Kishon

Tiberias

River Yarmuk

Nazareth

MT. TABOR
(1,843)

Gadara?

Nain

Esdraelon

River Jezreel

Caesarea

Scythopolis

MT. GILBOA
(1,696)

Decapolis

The Great Sea
(Mediterranean Sea)

Samaria

Samaria

Sychar

River Jordan

Gerasa

River Jabbok

MT. GERIZIM
(2,890)

Antipatris

Perea

Joppa

Arimathea

Ephraim

Gadara?

Philadelphia

Lydda

Emmaus

Jericho

Kirjath Jearim

Jerusalem

Bethabara

Beth Haccerem

Bethany

Qumran

Azotus

Bethlehem

Medeba

Ashkelon

Herodium

Gaza

Judea

Machaerus

Hebron

Dead Sea
(Salt Sea)
(-1,300)

River Arnon

Idumea

Masada

Beersheba

THE HOLY LAND
IN MODERN TIMES

Area occupied by Israel since June 1967

0   75 miles
0   75 kilometers

A   B   C   D   E

Tripoli

LEBANON

Beirut

BEKAA VALLEY

LEBANON MOUNTAINS

ANTI-LEBANON MOUNTAINS

Sidon

Damascus

SYRIA

Tyre

Dan

Qiryat Shemona

Quneitra

Nahariyya

**GOLAN
HEIGHTS**

Akko

Safad

1973 Line

Haifa

Tiberias

1967 Cease-Fire Line

*Sea of
Galilee*

Nazareth

Dera

Afula

Ramtha

Beth Shean

Hadera

Tulkarm

Netanya

Nablus

Jarash

Herzliyya

River Jordan

Tel Aviv
Yafo

Petah
Tiqwa

**WEST
BANK**

Rishon le Zion

Lod

Amman

Ramallah

Ramla

Ashdod

Jericho

Jerusalem

Ashqelon

Bethlehem

Madaba

Gaza

Qiryat
Gat

Hebron

Dhiban

**GAZA
STRIP**

En Gedi

*Dead Sea
(Salt Sea)*

Beersheba

Karak

Al-Arish

ISRAEL

JORDAN

Negev   *Arabah*

Sinai

*The Great Sea
(Mediterranean Sea)*

**SAUDI
ARABIA**

Elat

Aqaba

maps.com

© 2001 by Thomas Nelson, Inc.

79

Alphabetical List of Bible Books with Abbreviations Used in This Guide

Book	Abbreviation	Book	Abbreviation
Acts	Acts	1 Kings	1 Kgs
Amos	Am	2 Kings	2 Kgs
Baruch	Bar	Lamentations	Lam
1 Chronicles	1 Chr	Leviticus	Lv
2 Chronicles	2 Chr	Luke	Lk
Colossians	Col	1 Maccabees	1 Mc
1 Corinthians	1 Cor	2 Maccabees	2 Mc
2 Corinthians	2 Cor	Malachi	Mal
Daniel	Dn	Mark	Mk
Deuteronomy	Dt	Matthew	Mt
Ecclesiastes	Eccl	Micah	Mi
Ephesians	Eph	Nahum	Na
Esther	Est	Nehemiah	Neh
Exodus	Ex	Numbers	Nm
Ezekiel	Ez	Obadiah	Ob
Ezra	Ezr	1 Peter	1 Pt
Galatians	Gal	2 Peter	2 Pt
Genesis	Gn	Philemon	Phlm
Habakkuk	Hb	Philippians	Phil
Haggai	Hg	Proverbs	Prv
Hebrews	Heb	Psalms	Ps(s)
Hosea	Hos	Revelation	Rv
Isaiah	Is	Romans	Rom
James	Jas	Ruth	Ru
Jeremiah	Jer	1 Samuel	1 Sm
Job	Jb	2 Samuel	2 Sm
Joel	Jl	Sirach	Sir
1 John	1 Jn	Song of Songs	Song
2 John	2 Jn	1 Thessalonians	1 Thes
3 John	3 Jn	2 Thessalonians	2 Thes
John	Jn	1 Timothy	1 Tm
Jonah	Jon	2 Timothy	2 Tm
Joshua	Jos	Titus	Ti
Jude	Jude	Tobit	Tb
Judges	Jgs	Wisdom	Wis
Judith	Jdt	Zechariah	Zec
		Zephaniah	Zep

Glossary of Biblical and Related Terms

abba: From Aramaic—a language spoken in Palestine at the time of Jesus—*abba,* meaning "father," was used by children in addressing their fathers. Jesus used the word *abba* to express his relationship with God (Mk 14:36) and taught his disciples to pray to God as a loving and loveable parent.

Adam: Related to the Hebrew *adamah,* meaning "ground," this name signifies "one formed from the earth." According to the Book of Genesis, Adam was the first man to be formed; he was the husband of Eve and the father of Cain and Abel. In Catholic Church teaching, Christ is sometimes called the "new Adam" or the "second Adam," because Christ initiated the new or second creation by restoring the divine friendship that had been lost by original sin (1 Cor 15:45–49).

allegory: From the Greek *allegoria,* meaning "a description of one thing using the image of another," *allegory* refers to a form of biblical interpretation that finds symbolic meanings behind the literal text of the Scriptures; for example, the wandering of the Chosen People in the desert in search of the Promised Land is symbolically understood as the pilgrimage of a Christian toward heaven.

amen: From the Hebrew meaning "certainly" or "so be it" or "truly," *amen* is often used to signify assent at the end of a prayer or hymn. In the Gospels, Jesus used the word *amen* to introduce statements to emphasize their truth and authority.

anagogical sense: This word (from the Greek *anagein,* meaning "to refer") refers to a type of biblical interpretation that seeks the spiritual meaning of texts of the Scriptures; for example, Mary's acceptance at the Annunciation is seen as a paradigm of every Christian's vocation.

analogy: This word (from Greek *analogia,* meaning "proportion" or "resemblance") refers to a comparison of two objects that highlights their similarities, while acknowledging their differences. Analogy logically implies that if two things agree in some respects, they will probably agree in others.

angel: From the Greek *angelos,* meaning "messenger," *angel* refers to those spiritual beings who are both servants of God and messengers from God to people on earth. Such benevolent spirits are found not only in Christianity but also in Judaism, Islam, and other religions. According to medieval thought, angels were the last in a hierarchy of nine spiritual beings (seraphim, cherubim, thrones, dominations [or dominions], virtues, powers, principalities, archangels, and angels).

anointing: The word (from the Latin *inungere,* meaning "to smear" or "rub on" oil or ointment for medicinal purposes) refers to an act of applying oil in a religious ceremony or as part of a blessing. In the Old Testament, kings, priests, and prophets were anointed as a sign of their divine mission. Today, in the Catholic Church, anointing is part of the sacraments of Baptism, Confirmation, Holy Orders, and the Anointing of the Sick.

Antichrist: This word from the Greek literally means "against Christ," thus describing an adversary of Christ. In the New Testament, the Antichrist is a deceitful figure associated with the mystery of iniquity that is to precede the Second Coming of Christ. In modern usage, the term *Antichrist* describes both those who falsely claim to speak in the name of Christ and those who are enemies of Christ.

antithetical parallelism: This is a literary form used in Hebrew poetry that consists of a phrase or sentence followed by a phrase or sentence that is its opposite.

apocalypse: This word (from the Greek *apocalypsis,* meaning "revelation" or "unveiling" or "uncovering") in a general sense refers to the end of the world when God will destroy the forces of evil. In the Scriptures, the Apocalypse or Book of Revelation, which is the last book of the New Testament, describes the conflict between good and evil, the end of the world and heaven.

apocalyptic literature: Having roots in both Jewish and Christian tradition, this genre of literature appears in Ezekiel, Daniel, and Revelation. It is associated with the end-times or the last things and anticipates the time of final judgment when Jesus returns and the world as we know it disappears. Frequently referred to as "crisis literature," it generally appears in the context of historical, political, or religious turmoil and is characterized by symbols and images used to communicate a message to the intended audience while preventing the enemies of faith from understanding its true meaning.

apocrypha: This word (from the Greek *apokryphos,* meaning "hidden" or "obscure") refers to writings of questionable authorship or dubious authenticity. On the one hand, the term *apocrypha* is used to refer to those early Christian writings that were not included in the New Testament. On the other hand, the term *apocrypha* is used by Protestants to refer to those books of the Bible that are included in the Septuagint and the Vulgate but not in Hebrew or Protestant Bibles. Catholics refer to these books as deuterocanonical and consider them part of the canon of Scripture.

Apostle: The Greek word is *apostolos,* meaning "messenger," especially "a messenger who is sent on a mission." In the Gospels, the Apostles were chosen and sent on mission by Jesus, just as Jesus was sent by the Father, to preach the Gospel to the whole world. In addition to the original twelve Apostles, Paul and a few other people are also called Apostles in the New Testament.

apostolic succession: In Catholic teaching, apostolic succession refers to the continuous line of bishops who have succeeded to the ministry of the original twelve Apostles. While some privileges of the Apostles, especially their personal relationship with Jesus, could not be passed down, the Apostles did hand over to their successors the task of apostolic preaching and guiding the Church. The Catholic Church teaches that its bishops have by divine law taken the place of the Apostles as the pastors and leaders of the Church. (See also *Tradition.*)

Ascension: This word (from the Latin *ascendere,* meaning "to climb up") refers to Christ's being taken up bodily into heaven forty days after his Resurrection, to be seated at the right hand of the Father (see Mk 16:19, Lk 24:50–53).

Baal: This is a generic Semitic word meaning "master," "owner," "husband," or "lord." The word could be used to refer to Yahweh or to the master of a slave (Hos 2:16). However, in the Scriptures, the word *Baal* most often referred to the practices of idolatry or the worship of gods other than Yahweh. Baal was both the name of a specific god and a generic title that could refer to any number of gods such as Baal Peor or Baal of Hermon. Often the religion included the use of temple prostitutes and even demanded human sacrifice, especially of infants. The worshipers of Baal were generally seen as the enemies of the Israelites (1 Kgs 18:20–40).

Baptism: In Catholic teaching, this word (from the Greek *baptizein,* meaning "to immerse" or "to plunge") refers to the sacrament that washes away both original sin and personal sin. Baptism is the first and chief sacrament of the forgiveness of sins. Jesus, who was baptized by John the Baptist, instructed his disciples to preach the Gospel and baptize people in the name of the Father and the Son and the Holy Spirit (Mt 28:19). As one of the sacraments of Christian initiation in the Catholic Church, Baptism makes its recipients members of the Body of Christ, incorporates them into the Church, and empowers them to share in the mission of the Church.

Beatitudes: The Beatitudes are the blessings enunciated by Jesus as part of the Sermon on the Mount (Mt 5:3–12) and as part of the Sermon on the Plain (Lk 6:20–26). The Beatitudes are often considered to represent the heart of the preaching of Jesus.

Bible: This word (derived from the Greek *biblia,* meaning "books") refers to the collection of Jewish and Christian writings that are considered inspired and normative for belief. The Hebrew Bible contains many of the works of what Christians call the Old Testament; the Christian Bible also includes writings known as the New Testament. See *New Testament; Old Testament*

biblical criticism: This term (from the Greek *kritikos,* meaning "able to judge") refers to two different approaches to studying the Bible: (1) "lower criticism" attempts to reconstruct the original biblical text (because none of the original manuscripts have survived); (2) "higher criticism" compares this reconstructed text with other documents of the time.

biblical interpretation: Biblical interpretation looks at not only what the human authors intended to say but also what God reveals to humans through their words. Catholic Church criteria for interpreting the Scriptures are: (1) consider the kind of writing, that is, the literary form, in which a particular passage appears; (2) consider the context of each author's historical time and the presumptions that the author and the audience shared; and (3) consider the context of the process of revelation that occurred over time. Early insights often represent one step in understanding a mystery, not the fullness of revelation. The Catholic Church teaches that the Scriptures should be read and understood within the living Tradition of the Church. (See also *Tradition.*)

canon of Scripture: The canon of Scripture is the official list of the books of the Bible regarded as sacred because they are inspired; the list of books accepted by Catholic and Orthodox churches includes some books and parts of books not accepted as inspired by most Protestant churches.

Chosen People: According to the Old Testament, God chose Abraham and his descendants to be the recipients of divine revelation and so to play a unique role in salvation history; thus, their descendants, the Jewish people, are God's Chosen People.

Christ: This word comes from the Greek *christos,* meaning the "anointed one," and translates the Hebrew word *messiah.* In the Old Testament, kings, priests, and prophets were anointed; in giving Jesus the title "Christ," the New Testament indicates that Jesus fulfilled the messianic hope of Israel through his threefold office of king, prophet, and priest.

Christian: According to the Acts of the Apostles (11:26), the disciples of Jesus were first called Christians in Antioch. In accord with the Greek word *christos* (meaning the "anointed one"), a Christian is a person who has been anointed at Baptism and Confirmation. In contemporary usage, all those who profess to follow Christ are called Christians.

Christology: This word (a combination of "Christ" and the Greek *logos,* meaning "word" or "study") signifies the branch of theology that studies the person of Jesus Christ, his ministry, and mission. Theologians use the term *Christology from above* when referring to studies of Jesus that begin by reflecting on the pre-existent Word (logos) of God, and from that vantage point examine the implications of his assuming a human nature. They use the term *Christology from below* when referring to studies of Jesus that begin by reflecting on his human experiences, and from that vantage point discern the manifestations of his divinity.

circumcision: The word (from the Latin *circum,* meaning "around," and *cædere,* meaning "to cut") refers to the act of surgically removing the foreskin of males; according to Jewish Law, males are to be circumcised eight days after birth (Gn 17:12–14, Lv 12:3).

commandments of God: The commandments of God are the ten laws or Decalogue given by God to Moses on Mount Sinai (Ex 20:2–17, Dt 5:6–21) as the fundamental rules of conduct for the Chosen People. The first three of the Ten Commandments concern the love of God; the other seven commandments concern the love of neighbor.

contextualist: A contextualist interprets biblical passages by considering the literary and historical context and the whole process of revelation in order to correctly understand what the Bible is teaching.

councils of the Church: In the Catholic Church, this term (from the Latin *concilium,* meaning "meeting") refers to assemblies of bishops and other church leaders. The tradition of holding councils began with the Apostles in Jerusalem (Acts 15:1–35) and continues to the present.

Council of Trent (1545–1563): This general council of the Roman Catholic Church was held in the city of Trent (Italy), in response to the Protestant Reformation. This council addressed such central theological issues as the relationship of the Scriptures and Tradition and the doctrine of grace and the sacraments, confirmed the canon of the Scriptures in the Catholic Church, and set in motion the Counter-Reformation that would continue until the time of the Second Vatican Council.

covenant: This word (from the Latin *convenire,* meaning "to come together") refers to an agreement between two parties. The covenants between God and Israel are central to the Old Testament, where God promised to be faithful to the Chosen People who in turn were expected to observe God's commandments. The New Testament provides the definitive Covenant between God and the human race.

Creation accounts: Genesis, the first book of the Bible, presents two different accounts of God's Creation of all things (Gn 1:1—2:4 and Gn 2:4—3:24); although different in their details, both accounts present Creation as a divine action that affirms the goodness of all creatures:

in particular, humans were created in the image of God (Gn 1:27) and called to live in mutual and life-giving friendships (Gn 2:18–22).

Day of Atonement: See *Yom Kippur.*

deacon: In the Catholic Church, this word (from the Greek *diakonos,* meaning "servant") refers to one of the three Holy Orders; the other two are those of priest and bishop. The origin of the diaconate is customarily traced to the decision of the Apostles to deputize assistants to help with the material services of the Church (Acts 6:1–7).

Dead Sea scrolls: From the time of King David (1000 BCE), Jewish rebels and refugees sought shelter in the caves cut into the limestone cliffs along the left bank of the Dead Sea. The site had been a ruin since the Romans destroyed Jerusalem in 68–70 CE. In the spring of 1947, Bedouin shepherds found clay jars filled with ancient writings hidden by a group we call the Essenes. The find included the Dead Sea scrolls, a Hebrew canon of Scripture (except Esther) from 250 BCE, older than any Old Testament in existence by one thousand years. The Dead Sea scroll collection also included Essene writings in Hebrew, Aramaic, and Greek.

Decalogue: This word (from the Greek *deka,* meaning "ten," and *logos,* meaning "word") refers to the Ten Commandments revealed to Moses by God on Mount Sinai.

demon: This word comes from *daimon,* which in classical Greek refers to a "lesser god" or a "guiding spirit." In biblical Greek, however, *daimon* refers to an "unclean" or "evil spirit," especially in those who are possessed.

demythologization: This word (from the Latin *de,* meaning "from," and the Greek *mythos,* meaning "story" or "speech") refers to the attempt, associated with Rudolph Bultmann (1884–1976), to remove the mythical elements from the Bible so that the biblical message could be better understood by people living in the modern world.

deuterocanonical: This word (from the Greek *deuteros,* meaning "second," and *kanon,* meaning "rule") refers to those books of the Bible that are regarded as inspired by Roman Catholics and Eastern Christians, but not by Jews and Protestants. Roman Catholics consider the following books deuterocanonical: Tobit, Judith, 1 and 2 Maccabees, Wisdom, Sirach (or Ecclesiasticus), Baruch, plus parts of Esther and Daniel.

deuteronomist: This term is used for the person or group responsible for writing the histories contained in the Old Testament books of Deuteronomy through 2 Kings. The deuteronomist emphasized that God's just punishment occurred whenever the people sinned and broke their covenant with God. The deuteronomist also emphasized that if the people repented and returned to obedience to the Law of Moses, God's favor would return.

Diaspora: This word (from the Greek *diaspeirein,* meaning "to scatter") refers to a community of people who live in exile from their native land. In the Old Testament, the Diaspora of the Jewish people began in 587 BCE when the Temple in Jerusalem was destroyed and many Jews were taken into exile in Babylon.

disciple: This word (from the Latin *discipulus,* meaning "pupil") refers to the original followers of Christ and, by extension, to all those who try to follow the teaching of Christ.

dispersion: See *Diaspora.*

dynamic equivalence: This approach to Bible translation attempts to recast the meaning of the original language of the scriptural text into natural, modern English, with little regard for the structure or specific vocabulary of the original language.

Elohim: Elohim is one of the names for God in the Old Testament. Some scholars translate the word in the plural to mean "divinities" or "host of heaven"; other scholars consider Elohim a "majestic plural."

Elohist: The scribes who wrote of Elohim were the Elohists. They lived in seventh- to sixth-century BCE. Later writers edited the Elohists' writings into sections of the Pentateuch. Referred to by scholars as the E Tradition, the scribes portray God as a humanlike figure who appears in person at different events and who is capable of regret.

Emmanuel: This word from the Hebrew means "God with us." Matthew's Gospel calls Jesus by the name Emmanuel (1:23).

epistle: This word (from the Greek *epistole,* meaning "message" or "letter") refers to the letters written by Church leaders in the first two centuries CE, especially those letters that are included in the New Testament and, in the Catholic Church, read during the celebration of the Mass and other sacraments.

eschatology: This word (from the Greek *eschatos,* meaning "last" or "remote," and *logos,* meaning "word" or "study") refers to the theological study of the last things: death and judgment, heaven and hell, the end of the world, the recapitulation of all in God, and so on.

Essenes: The origin of this word is uncertain; the Essenes were members of a Jewish sect at the time of Jesus who lived an ascetic life in the solitude of the desert near the Dead Sea.

etiology: This is a narrative that is intended to explain the origin or cause of some social custom, natural phenomenon, or religious ritual. Etiologies are also used to explain the origin of names and places.

E Tradition: See *Elohist.*

Eucharist, the: In the Catholic Church, this word (from the Greek *eucharistia,* meaning "thanksgiving" or "gratitude") sometimes refers to the celebration of the entire Mass and sometimes specifically to the consecrated bread and wine that have become the Body and Blood of Christ.

evangelist: This word (from the Greek *eu,* meaning "good," and *angelos,* meaning "messenger") refers to those who spread the Evangel or Gospel (Good News) of Christ. *Evangelist* has two meanings: (1) the New Testament authors who wrote the Gospels of Matthew, Mark, Luke, and John; and (2) anyone who evangelizes or preaches the Gospel.

Eve: This name (related to the Hebrew *hawwah,* meaning "a living being") is given to the first woman, who was the partner of Adam and the mother of Cain and Abel (Gn chaps. 2–4). In Catholic teaching, Mary is sometimes called the "new Eve" or the "second Eve," because, as Mother of God, she was instrumental in initiating the new or second creation.

exegesis: This word (from the Greek *exegeisthai,* meaning "to explain" or "to interpret") refers to the critical explanation of a text, especially the grammatical and structural analysis of biblical texts.

exile: This word (from the Latin *exilium,* meaning "banishment") refers to an absence from one's native land; sometimes this separation is forced; at other times it is self-imposed or voluntary. The Babylonian Exile (587–539 BCE) was a particularly symbolic part of Jewish history; the Catholic Church today considers itself in exile until the coming of the risen Lord.

Exodus: This Greek word meaning "going out" is the name given to the second book of the Bible, which describes the departure of the Israelites from Egypt under the leadership of Moses. The Exodus is celebrated at Passover as the liberation of the Chosen People.

Fall, the: The Fall is a theological term referring to the account of Genesis (chap. 3) that explains the presence of evil and death in the world as the result of a double Fall—the sin of some of the angels and the sin of Adam and Eve.

Father: Jesus called God "abba" (Father) and taught his disciples to pray to God as "our Father." Although many other religions look upon God as Father, Christianity views God the Father as a person of the blessed Trinity.

formal equivalence: This approach to Bible translation is a literal interpretation of the original language of the text of the Scriptures. It strives to stay close to the vocabulary, structure, and even word order of the original Hebrew, Aramaic, or Greek. The goal is to allow the reader who does not know these languages to gain some sense of the original wording.

form criticism: Form criticism (or *Formgeschichte* in German) is a method of studying the literary forms of a document in order to ascertain the background of a particular passage. For example, biblical form criticism studies such forms as parables, proverbs, and poems in order to discover the origin and history of a particular scriptural text.

fundamentalism: This term (from the Latin *fundamentum,* meaning "foundation") has three different but related senses: (1) the five foundational principles that have been adopted by many Protestants: (a) the inerrancy of the Scriptures, (b) the virgin birth and the divinity of Christ, (c) Christ's death as an atonement for sin, (d) the bodily Resurrection of Christ, and (e) Christ's imminent return; (2) a belief in the absolute inerrancy of the Scriptures along with a rejection of the historical critical method; (3) any type of scriptural interpretation that is extremely literal, for example, Islamic fundamentalism.

Gehenna: This word (from the Hebrew *Ge Hinnom,* meaning the "valley of Hinnom") was the name of the place where children were once sacrificed to Molech (Jer 19:5); Jesus spoke of Gehenna as a place of punishment for those who refused to repent and be converted.

genre: A genre is a category of literature, art, or music. Genres in the Scriptures include prose, poetry, myth, law codes, historical narrative, didactic (teaching) narrative, parable, and miracle stories. The first step in correctly interpreting a scriptural passage is to know its genre.

Gentile: This word (from the Latin *gens,* meaning "race" or "clan") is usually used in the New Testament to designate a person who is not Jewish; sometimes the word is used to refer to a person who is not Christian.

gospel: This word (from the Old English *god,* meaning "good," and *spel,* meaning "story" or "message") is a translation of the Greek *euangelion,* meaning "good news"; the New Testament uses the term *Good News* or *Gospel* to refer both to the message of Jesus and to the four books written about his life and death: Matthew, Mark, Luke, and John.

grace: This word (from the Latin *gratia,* meaning "pleasant quality" or "goodwill") refers to a free and undeserved supernatural help that God gives persons so that they may respond to the divine call to salvation.

heaven: From the Old English meaning "home of God," *heaven* has various meanings: (1) in the ancient world, heaven was often identified with the sky or firmament and considered the dwelling place of the divine; (2) in Judaism, because of the reluctance to pronounce the name of God, heaven was sometimes used as a substitute for God's name; (3) among Christians, heaven represents the final goal of all Christians where they are definitively united with God and reunited with their fellow Christians.

Hebrew: This word of Hebrew origin seemingly meant "one from the other side" or possibly "immigrant." The word *Hebrew* can refer to either the Israelite people or their language.

Hellenism: This word refers to the acceptance of Greek culture, language, and traditions. After Alexander the Great conquered the Mediterranean Sea and Middle Eastern world, his reign resulted in Greek culture, religion, customs, and language being spread across the West. This Hellenization lasted six hundred years. One result was the translation of the Hebrew Scriptures into the Greek language, a version called the Septuagint. The New Testament was written in Greek because of the influence of Hellenism. See also *Septuagint.*

hermeneutics: This word (from the Greek *hermeneus,* meaning "interpreter") refers to the study of the interpretation of texts, especially, the study of the theory and method of biblical interpretation.

high place: Both the Hebrews and the Canaanites established places of worship on high ground (Gn 12:7–8, 1 Kgs 13:32). The Caananite high places often included practices of the fertility rites and human sacrifices offered to Baal Molech and Asherah. Over the centuries, the Hebrews destroyed the high places of the Canaanites (Dt 12:2–3).

historical critical method: This term (from the Greek *historia,* meaning "record" or "account," and *kritikos,* meaning "able to judge") refers to a method of studying texts, especially the Bible. The historical critical method considers the historical context, the philosophical presuppositions, and the theological perspective of a particular passage. See also *biblical criticism.*

holy of holies: The holy of holies, the innermost part of the Temple in Jerusalem, was the repository for the ark of the Covenant; only the high priest was permitted to enter the holy of holies and then only once a year.

Holy Spirit: This word (from the Latin *spiritus,* meaning "breath" or "soul") refers to the third person of the Trinity, the Paraclete divinely sent to teach and guide the Church to the end of times. See also *Paraclete.*

idolatry: This word (from the Greek *eidolon,* meaning "image," and *latreia,* meaning "worship") refers to the worship of images, creatures, or created things—idols—in place of God. Idolatry, which is a divinization of creatures, is a sin against the first commandment (Ex 20:3, Dt 5:7).

Incarnation: This word (from the Latin *in,* meaning "in," and *caro,* meaning "flesh") refers to the central Christian belief that the Son of God assumed human nature and, as stated in the Nicene Creed, "became flesh and dwelt among us."

inerrancy: This word (from the Latin *in,* meaning "not," and *error,* meaning "mistake" or "going astray") in the Catholic tradition refers to the belief that the Scriptures teach faithfully and without error the salvific message intended by God. Some fundamentalists understand inerrancy to mean that the Bible does not contain any errors, not only in regard to faith and morals, but in all matters, including history, science, and so on.

inspiration: This word (from the Latin *inspirare,* meaning "to breathe into") refers to the divine assistance of the Holy Spirit given to the authors of the books of the Bible. Gifted with this divine assistance, the biblical authors were enabled to write in human words the salvific message that God wanted to communicate.

Israel: This name comes from Jacob's experience of "wrestling with God" (Gn 32:28) and is used in different ways: (1) for the twelve Tribes of Israel as descendants of the twelve sons of Jacob; (2) for the Chosen People or Jewish People as a whole; (3) for the northern kingdom (Israel) in contrast to the southern kingdom (Judah); (4) for the modern nation of Israel.

Jesus Christ: This name, combining the Hebrew *Yeshua,* meaning "God saves," and the Greek *christos,* meaning "anointed one," refers to both the Jesus of history and the Christ of faith (Mk 14:61).

J Tradition: See *Yahwist.*

jubilee: This word comes from the sound of the ram's horn trumpet, the shofar. When blown, the shofar's sound signified the heavens opening and the presence of God made near. According to the Law of Moses, every fiftieth year was proclaimed a jubilee, a year of repentance, and the people were to place their focus on the redistribution of wealth and property to the poor and dispossessed. During the jubilee, the land was to rest. Only gleaning of the fields was permitted. All landed property was returned to its original owners, slaves were set free, and all debts were erased (Lv 25:8–55). The jubilee created a society of justice in which the bounty and the land were shared. It prevented abject poverty and erased lines between rich and poor. It corrected societal injustices and restored God's intended equality to human relationships.

Judah, Judea: These words came from the Hebrew word *Yehudah,* meaning "praise the Lord." Judah was a son of Jacob and Leah, a patriarch and founder of one of the twelve Tribes of Israel. The tribe of Judah became the most powerful of the twelve Tribes. Judah became a place-name of the southern territory of Palestine. Judah and its capital city, Jerusalem, were the headquarters for the administration of the nation of Israel, the location of religious life via the Temple, and the dwelling place of the royal family of David. For centuries, the Temple priests and Judean kings ruled Judah. In the time of Roman rule, the area was called Judea.

Judaism: This word, which has been traced to Judah, the fourth son of Jacob and the tribe descended from him, refers to the monotheistic religion of the Jewish people who trace their origin to Abraham and whose religious observance is based on the Torah and the Talmud.

judgment, final: This term (from the Latin *judicare,* meaning "to judge," and *finis,* meaning "end") refers to Christ's judgment at the end of time, when each person's acceptance or refusal of grace will be made known.

Kingdom of God: The word *kingdom* is a translation of the Greek *basileia,* which may also be translated "kingship" or "reign." The Kingdom of God is at the center of the preaching of Jesus, who taught his disciples to pray for the coming of the Kingdom in the Our Father. The messianic kingdom, which is inaugurated by Jesus, will triumph over Satan at the end of time.

kingdom of heaven: The Gospel of Matthew uses the expression *kingdom of heaven,* which seemingly reflects the Jewish custom of not speaking directly about God or the Kingdom of God.

Last Judgment: See *judgment, final.*

Law (Biblical): The Law or Torah, comprising the first five books of the Bible, is contrasted with the books of the Prophets and the other Writings. In the New Testament, Jesus often referred to "the Law and the Prophets." See *Tanak.*

law of the Gospel: See *Law (New).*

Law (New): The New Law refers to those commandments or the way of life taught by Jesus Christ in fulfillment of the Old Law.

Law (Old): Christians consider the Law of Moses to be the first stage of revealed law and so the preparation for the Gospel. See *Torah; Pentateuech; Law (Biblical).*

Levi, Levite: One of Leah's sons fathered by Jacob (Gn 29:34), Levi became a patriarch of Israel and the head of the tribe that carried his name, also called Levites. Moses and Aaron were descendants of Levi (Ex 2:1). According to the command of God, only Aaron and his sons could serve as priests (Ex 28:1). Thus, the Levites became the tribe entrusted with sacred ministries, the caretakers of the tabernacle and the Temple (Nm 1:48–54). See *priest; sacrifice.*

literal sense: This term (from the Latin *litera,* meaning "letter") refers to a form of biblical interpretation that translates a text word-for-word and emphasizes the explicit meaning of biblical texts. See *senses of the Scriptures.*

literary criticism: This term refers to a method of studying the Scriptures that looks at the text and seeks to understand it as a work of literature. Literary criticism considers what literary form (e.g., a poem, a letter, a story) or device (e.g., puns, parables, exaggerations) was used and how that particular literary form or device functioned in an ancient society. See *exegesis.*

literary forms: Literary forms are categories of smaller units of text that can be used within a particular genre. For example, the newspaper genre contains many literary forms, including national news stories, editorials, obituaries, sports stories, and classified ads.

logos: This Greek word has a variety of meanings: "word," "reason," "discourse," and so on. In ancient Greek thought, for example, the *logos* was the principle of reason and order in the world. In the prologue to the Gospel According to John, the word *logos* refers to the second person of the Trinity become man in Jesus Christ.

Lord: This word (from the Old English for "ruler" or "master of a household") is used in the Bible to refer to God in the Old Testament and primarily to Jesus Christ in the New Testament as an affirmation of his divinity.

messiah: This word comes from the Hebrew *mashah,* meaning "anoint," and was later translated into Greek as *christos* and into English as Christ. Many of the Jewish contemporaries of Jesus were awaiting the arrival of a messiah to deliver them from oppression.

messianic secret: This phrase refers to a theme in the Gospel of Mark that portrays Jesus' disciples as recognizing his identity as the Messiah; however, Jesus directed them not to tell anyone else.

metaphor: This word (from the Greek *metaphora,* meaning "transfer") refers to a literary comparison that compares and contrasts two things that are basically different. The parables of Jesus, for example, describe the Kingdom of God by using human examples that are different from, but simultaneously suggest the uniqueness of, the Kingdom.

millennialism: This word (from the Latin *mille,* meaning "thousand," and *annus,* meaning "year") refers to the expectation of a thousand-year reign of Christ based on the Book of Revelation (20:2–7); because this passage has been interpreted in a wide variety of ways, there are many different forms of millennialism.

miracle: This word (from the Latin *miraculum,* meaning "an object of wonder") generically describes a marvelous and unexpected event that manifests the presence and power of God. The word *miracle* does not appear in the New Testament; what are traditionally called the "miracles of Jesus" were described as "mighty deeds" and "signs" that point to the presence of the Kingdom of God.

Mosaic Law: See *Law (Old).*

Mount Zion: This was the hill on which the citadel of David and the city of Jerusalem stood. On Zion, David built his palace and Solomon later built the Temple of Jerusalem. The city of Jerusalem came to represent the people and faith of Israel (Pss 87:2, 149:2). In the Scriptures, the use of the phrase "virgin Zion" represented the ideal, pure relationship between the people of Israel and God (2 Kgs 19:21, Lam 2:13–22). During the Babylonian Captivity (586–539 BCE), the prophets promised a time when God would make his home again in Zion (Zec 2:10–11). In the Book of Revelation, Jesus Christ, the lamb of God, appeared on Mount Zion (Rv 14:1).

myth: This word (from the Greek *mythos,* meaning "story" or "speech") is used in a variety of ways: (1) originally, a myth was a story about the gods or heavenly beings and usually taught a moral lesson; (2) theologians sometimes contrast fact and myth understood as a story that is not factual but artificially contrived to teach a lesson; (3) myth has been understood as a story of ultimate significance that treats the origin, purpose, and end of creatures and creation.

New Covenant: This term refers to the covenant or law established by God in order to fulfill and perfect the Old Covenant or Mosaic Law; the Second Vatican Council emphasized that the New Covenant does not replace the Old Covenant, much less does it oppose the Old Covenant; rather it brings the Old Covenant to completion. See *Law (New); Law (Old); Old Covenant.*

New Testament: This term refers to the biblical writings that were circulated within the early Christian communities and that narrated the life, death, and Resurrection of Christ and the work of the Holy Spirit within the life of these communities; these writings were later accepted by the Church as divinely inspired.

Old Covenant: This term refers to the Covenant or Law that was given by God to Moses on Mount Sinai for the Chosen People. Although Christians consider the Old Law a preparation for the New Covenant or New Law given by Christ, the Old Covenant has never been revoked. See *Law (New); Law (Old); New Covenant.*

Old Testament: This term is the Christian name for those biblical writings that record God's revelation to the Chosen People. Christians believe that the Old Testament anticipates and prepares for the New Testament, which is accordingly the culmination and completion of the Old Testament. See *Septuagint; Tanak.*

oracle: These are brief, poetic utterances that contain a message or pronouncement from God.

original grace, original righteousness: This word (from the Latin *origo,* meaning "beginning" or "birth") refers to the state of blessedness and perfection associated with Adam and Eve before their transgression.

original sin: This term (from the Latin *origo,* meaning "beginning" or "birth") refers to the sin of the first human beings who disobeyed God's command and thereby lost their original holiness and became subject to death. Original sin is transmitted to every person born into the world.

parable: This word, which comes from the Greek *parabole,* meaning "comparison," is a short story that uses everyday images to communicate a religious message. Jesus used parables frequently in his teaching and preaching as a way of presenting the Gospel or Good News of salvation.

Paraclete: This word (from the Greek *parakletos,* meaning "advocate" or "helper") is used in the Gospel of John to describe the Holy Spirit, who was promised to the disciples as an advocate or consoler. See also *Holy Spirit.*

paradise: This word (from the Greek *paradeisos,* meaning "park" or "paradise") refers both to the Garden of Eden in the Book of Genesis and also to the New Jerusalem in the Book of Revelation and has come to be identified with heaven.

Parousia: This Greek word, meaning "arrival" or "presence," refers to the Second Coming of Christ or the return of Christ in glory to judge the living and the dead at the end of the world. See *Second Coming of Christ.*

Paschal lamb: This term comes from the Greek *pascha,* meaning "Passover," the Jewish celebration at which a lamb was sacrificed and eaten in commemoration of God's deliverance of the Chosen People from bondage in Egypt. The Gospel of John (19:14) portrays Jesus as the lamb of God who is sacrificed on the cross for the redemption of all people.

Passion of Christ: This term (from the Latin *passio,* meaning "suffering") refers to the sufferings of Jesus during the final days in his life: his agony in the garden of Gethsemane, his trial, and his Crucifixion. Contemporary theologians often relate the Passion of Christ to the present-day suffering of people, especially the needy and marginalized.

Passover: This was the Jewish feast memorializing the Exodus from Egypt when the Hebrews sacrificed a lamb, smeared its blood on their doorposts, prepared unleavened bread, bitter herbs, and the wine of blessing, and shared the sacred seder meal as family. That night, the Lord passed over the houses of Egypt, and in all the houses not marked with the blood of the lamb, the firstborn children and animals died (Ex 21:29–30). Pharaoh sent the Israelites away. They crossed the Red Sea and became a free people.

The Passover festival with its seder meal and its Paschal lamb commemorate the creation of a new people, a society of justice based on a sacred trust between Yahweh and Israel. Passover honors a God who heard the cries of his people and responded with miraculous power to free them from a terrible oppressor. Jesus gathered his disciples together on Passover to celebrate the seder and offer them the bread of life (Mt 26:17–30; Mk 14:12–26; Lk 22:7–23; 1 Cor 10:1, 11:23–26). See also *Eucharist; Exodus; Paschal lamb.*

patriarch (Old Testament): This word (from the Greek *patriarches,* meaning "chief" or "head of a family") is a title given to the fathers of the Old Testament, such as Abraham, Isaac, and Jacob, who were divinely selected to guide the Chosen People.

Pentateuch: This word (from the Greek *pente,* meaning "five," and *teuchos,* meaning "vessel" or "container for scrolls") is a name given to the Torah, the first five books of the Hebrew Scriptures: Genesis, Exodus, Leviticus, Numbers, and Deuteronomy. See *Old Testament; Torah.*

personification: This is the giving of human attributes to an idea or abstract concept.

Pentecost: This word (from the Greek *pentekoste hemera,* meaning "fiftieth day") was originally the Hellenistic term for the Jewish feast of Weeks. For Christians, Pentecost, which is celebrated seven weeks after Easter, commemorates the descent of the Holy Spirit upon the disciples who were empowered to preach the Gospel, and so marks the beginning of the Church (Acts 2:1–13).

Pharisees: This word (from the Hebrew *parash,* meaning "to separate") designates a Jewish religious party or school at the time of Jesus. The Pharisees, who faithfully adhered to the Mosaic Law and believed in the resurrection of the body, are depicted in the New Testament as hostile to the teaching of Jesus.

preferential option for the poor: This biblically based phrase, redefined in the *Catechism of the Catholic Church* as preferential love for the poor (no. 2448), is a central concept in Catholic social teaching, which, following the example of Jesus, seeks justice for the poor, oppressed, marginalized, and so on. This phrase, which has many antecedents in both the Bible and Catholic Church teaching, received considerable attention at the conference of Latin American bishops in 1979 at Puebla, Mexico.

priest: This word (from the Greek *presbyter,* meaning "elder") in the Scriptures designates one who offers sacrifice to God on behalf of the people. The first priestly man in the Hebrew tradition was Melchizedek of Salem. With Abraham, he offered bread and wine and was a "priest of God Most High" (Gn 14:18). As part of the Sinai Covenant, God instituted an order of priests that began with Aaron and his sons. Because they were of the tribe of Levi, the Levites became known as the priestly class. As the Israelites settled Palestine, they built local temples at which the priests led the community in prayer and offered required animal sacrifices.

Once the Temple was built in Jerusalem, religious observances became centered there. All local temples were destroyed, and the priests were all moved to Jerusalem, where they assisted with worship and sacrifice in the Temple. The high priest was the chief priest and led all the major religious rituals in the Temple. The priesthood of Christ fulfills the expectations of the Old Testament priesthood through Christ's perfect sacrifice on the cross (Heb 7:1–28).

In the early Church, the role of priests took time to evolve. The first Christians gathered in people's homes to celebrate the Eucharist. An elder in the community often led these gatherings. The presbyters became known as priests, and their role evolved as taking their authority from the local bishop to lead the community in the sacrifice of the Mass and other sacraments. See *Levi, Levite.*

Priestly Tradition: This particular theological tradition present in the Pentateuch is the work of priestly scribes who hoped to restore the memory of the divided kingdoms of Israel and Judah and restore focus on the Sinai Covenant. Commonly known by scholars as the P Tradition, the scribes blended the names from northern Israel and southern Judah into a unified title for the Holy. Whenever the unspeakable name Yahweh was intended, the scribes used the honorable title *Adonai* with the generic *El* and called the Holy One "Adonai Yahweh Elohim." In English, this translates as "Lord God." God is portrayed as transcendent and distant, and thus the need for priestly intercession.

Promised Land: This term refers to the land that God promised to the descendants of Abraham (Gn chap. 12), the land of Canaan or Palestine.

prooftexting: This describes a verse from the Scriptures being wrenched from its context to make a point. Prooftexting fails to respect the way in which God's word is expressed in human language and ignores the particularity in which and by which God reveals.

prophecy: This word (from the Greek *propheteia,* meaning "the gift of interpreting the divine will") refers to the messages communicated by prophets on behalf of God. Prophecy is usually focused on the present through messages of divine direction or consolation; however, insofar as some prophetic messages include divine direction, their fulfillment may be in the future.

prophet: This word (from the Greek *prohetes,* meaning "interpreter" or "spokesperson") refers to a person chosen by God to communicate a salvific message. A biblical prophet was primarily a communicator of a divine message of repentance to the Chosen People and not necessarily a person who predicted the future.

proverb: This word (from the Latin *proverbium,* meaning "common saying") refers to any short saying that has been orally passed down as advice from generation to generation. The Book of Proverbs in the Old Testament contains many examples of such wisdom sayings, which provide an understanding of human experience from a religious perspective.

psalm, psalter: The word *psalm* (from the Greek *psalmos,* meaning "a song sung to a harp") refers to a hymn or song of prayer that expresses praise, thanksgiving, petition, lamentation, or a historical memory of God's actions on behalf of the Chosen People. The word *psalter* (from the Greek *psallein,* meaning "to play a stringed instrument") refers to the Book of Psalms in the Old Testament that contains one hundred fifty psalms.

pseudonymous: This is the literary practice of attributing a text to a well-known person (usually deceased) as a way to give the written work authority or to continue the tradition of an admired leader.

P Tradition: See *Priestly Tradition.*

Q source: This is a collection of ancient documents of the teachings of Jesus shared among the early followers of Christianity. Scholars believe that the Evangelists Matthew and Luke used this collection, also called the sayings of Jesus, in creating their Gospels. The collection is called the Q, or Quelle, source. *Quelle* is a German word meaning "source" or "spring." See *Synoptic Gospels.*

redaction criticism: This is a term (from the Latin *redigere,* meaning "to bring back" or "to collect") that refers to the process of editing or revising a text. Redaction criticism (or *Redaktionsgeschichte* in German) is the technical effort to determine the editorial history of a particular text, especially in biblical studies.

Resurrection of Christ: The Resurrection of Christ (from the Latin *resurgere,* meaning "to rise again") refers to the bodily rising of Jesus from the dead on the third day after his death on the cross and his burial in the tomb. Celebrated at Easter, it is the central mystery of the Christian faith.

resurrection of the dead: The resurrection of the dead refers to the raising of the just who will live forever with the risen Christ. The resurrection of the dead, which is mentioned in the Nicene Creed, is an essential part of Christian faith (1 Cor 15:1–23).

revelation: This word (from the Latin *revelare,* meaning "to unveil" or "to disclose") refers to the unveiling or self-manifestation of God and God's divine plan of salvation, through the prophets in the Old Testament and through Jesus Christ in the New Testament.

Sabbath, *Shabbath:* In the Old Testament, this Hebrew word refers to the "day of rest," the seventh day of the week, when, according to the Book of Genesis (2:1–3), God finished the work of Creation. For most Christians, Sunday, the day of the Resurrection, is observed as the day of rest and worship.

sacrifice: This word (from the Latin *sacer,* meaning "sacred," and *facere,* meaning "to make") refers to an offering made to God by a priest on behalf of the people as a sign of adoration, thanksgiving, petition, and communion (Lv chaps. 1–7). In the Old Testament, a sacrifice was needed as atonement, that is, a healing rite that restored holiness by cleansing the people from infractions of the Law. Sacrifices also reconciled the people's covenant relationship with God (Ps 51:1–17).

The only perfect sacrifice is that offered by Christ on the cross (Heb 7:22–28).

Sadducees: This term (whose origin is unclear) refers to a Jewish religious party or school at the time of Jesus; the Sadducees, who did not believe in the resurrection of the body, are depicted in the New Testament as hostile to the teaching of Jesus.

salvation history: This term refers to an interpretation of the Bible as a historical record of divine salvation. According to Christian teaching, God began disclosing this divine plan of salvation at the time of creation and continued revealing this plan through the historical events of the Old Testament, culminating with its definitive manifestation through Christ in the New Testament.

Samaria: This territory, whose name comes from Shemer, the owner of the hill on which the town was originally constructed (1 Kgs 16:24), consisted, at the time of Jesus, of the region south of Galilee and north of Judea, that is, the region between Nazareth and Jerusalem.

Samaritans: This term refers to the inhabitants of Samaria. The Samaritans rejected the Jerusalem Temple and worshiped at Mount Gerizim. The New Testament describes the Jewish rejection of Samaritans in both the parable of the good Samaritan (Lk 10:29–37) and the account of Jesus speaking with the Samaritan woman at the well (Jn 4:1–42).

Satan: This Hebrew word, meaning "adversary," refers to the fallen angel or spirit of evil, who is the enemy of God and a continuing instigator of temptation and sin in the world.

Savior: This word (from the Latin *salvator,* meaning "saver" or "preserver") is a title appropriately given to Jesus, whose Hebrew name means "God saves."

scribes: This word (from the Latin *scriba,* meaning "secretary" or "accountant") at the time of the New Testament referred to Jewish legal scholars or teachers of Jewish Law, who are often portrayed as opposed to Jesus.

Scriptures: This word (from the Latin *scribere,* "to write") refers to the Bible. The Scriptures are described as "sacred" insofar as they are divinely inspired; the Scriptures are described as "canonical" insofar as the list of the books of the Old and New Testaments has been officially determined by the Church.

Scriptures and Tradition: This term refers to the Catholic Church teaching that the revelation given by Jesus Christ to his Apostles has been transmitted in two forms: (1) the oral tradition that began with the Apostles and has continued through the centuries under the guidance of the Holy Spirit; (2) the written account of this revelation that has been recorded in the Bible. The Scriptures and Tradition are mutually related. Tradition gave birth to the Scriptures and is always necessary in order to interpret the Scriptures; the Scriptures in turn are the text that definitively expresses the tradition inherited from apostolic preaching.

Second Coming of Christ: This term refers to the Parousia, which will mark the culmination of history and the fulfillment of all creation. See *Parousia.*

Semitic: The ancient language, culture, and various racial groups that make up the Middle East all have a common Semitic ancestry. The Hebrew, Aramaic, Arabic, and Akkadian languages, as well as the lost Hyksos language of Egypt, all have a Semitic source or root.

senses of the Scriptures: This term indicates that every text is open to a variety of interpretations or senses. In the history of Christian biblical interpretation, the following meanings or senses of the Scriptures have been proposed: (1) the literal sense seeks the word-for-word meaning of a text; (2) the allegorical sense seeks the symbolic meaning behind the text; (3) the anagogical sense seeks the spiritual meaning of a text; (4) the tropological sense searches for the ethical implications of a text; (5) the typological sense shows how the Old Testament prefigured the New Testament.

Septuagint: This term (from the Latin *septuaginta,* meaning "seventy") is the name given to the Greek translation of the Hebrew Bible that was widely used among Hellenized Jews at the time of Jesus. According to a popular legend, a group of seventy (or 72) Jewish scholars, working independently, produced the same identical translation in seventy (or 72) days; hence the name "Septuagint" (seventy). See *Old Testament; Torah.*

simile: A simile is a literary form that makes comparisons using *like* or *as.*

soteriology: This word (from the Greek *soteria,* meaning "salvation," and *logos,* meaning "study") refers to the theological study of the doctrine of salvation. Soteriology traditionally has included the biblical ideas of Yahweh as the savior of Israel and Jesus as the Savior of the world; more recently, some theologians have included liberation from oppression under the heading of soteriology.

source criticism: This term refers to the method of studying the Scriptures that identifies other writings outside of the Scriptures known in the ancient cultures that influenced the writer of a specific passage. It considers whether the writers build on an existing story, myth, or other literature as a basis for their work and whether the theology or justice ethic of the biblical version varies from that of the cultural source. See *exegesis.*

synagogue: This word (from the Greek *synagoge,* meaning "meeting" or "assembly") refers to the worship assemblies of Jews who lived outside of Jerusalem as they gathered to celebrate the Sabbath; Jesus is depicted in the Gospel of Luke (4:14–30) as beginning his Galilean ministry in the synagogue at Nazareth.

synonymous parallelism: This is a literary form used in Hebrew poetry that consists of a phrase or sentence followed by a phrase or sentence that has the same meaning, even in each of its parts.

Synoptic Gospels: This term (from the Greek *syn,* meaning "together," and *horan,* meaning "to see") refers to the fact that the Gospels of Matthew, Mark, and Luke follow a similar pattern in both their overall structure and their individual narratives.

Synoptic Problem: This term refers to the task of providing an explanation of the historical relationship and common source of the Synoptic Gospels, which have a similar structure and include many of the same narratives.

synthetic parallelism: This is a literary form that consists of two lines of text, the first of which is completed by the second.

tabernacle: This word (from the Latin *tabernaculum,* meaning "tent," especially a tent used for religious purposes) refers in the Old Testament to the portable tent that was used as a sanctuary for the ark of the Covenant during the Chosen People's migration in the desert and before the building of the Temple in Jerusalem.

Talmud: This Hebrew word meaning "instruction" refers to the collection of rabbinic writings that constitute the basic religious authority in Judaism.

Tanak: This word is an acronym that refers to the major divisions of the Hebrew Scriptures: *Torah* (Law–T), *Nebi'im* (Prophets–N), and *Kethuyim* (Writings–K).

teaching of contempt: This term was coined by the French historian Jules Isaac to mean the long legacy of Christian teaching and preaching that disparaged Jews and Judaism. Centuries of anti-Jewish teaching and preaching were key factors in Christian complicity in the Shoah (Holocaust).

temples: This biblical term refers to the various temples mentioned in the Old Testament. The Jewish people built temples on Mount Moriah, believed to be the place where Isaac went to sacrifice Jacob (Gn chap. 22). The so-called First Temple period (1006–586 BCE) began with David's occupation of Jerusalem and was followed by Solomon's building the First Temple; this period ended with the Babylonian Exile. The Second Temple period (536 BCE–70 CE) began with the return of the Jewish exiles and culminated in the building of a new temple by Herod shortly before the birth of Jesus; this temple was destroyed by the Romans about four decades after the death of Jesus.

testament: This word (from the Latin *testamentum,* meaning "will") describes the two parts of the Bible, the Old Testament and the New Testament, both of which are covenants offered by God.

textual criticism: "This term refers to a method of studying the Scriptures that seeks to determine, as accurately as possible, the original wording of a given passage in the original language. Thousands of ancient, hand-written copies ("manuscripts") of different parts of the Bible have survived, and they typically have a number of differences between them, usually the result of copyists' errors. Textual critics compare these differences (called "variant readings") to determine which variant is likely to be the actual wording of the original author. The result is called a "critical text." All reputable modern translations of the Bible, including the New American Bible, the Jerusalem Bible, and the New Revised Standard Bible, are based on critical texts.

Torah: This word (from the Hebrew *torah,* meaning "law" or "instruction") refers to the Pentateuch or the Mosaic Law, which includes the first five books of the Hebrew Scriptures: Genesis, Exodus, Leviticus, Numbers, and Deuteronomy. See *Old Testament; Tanak.*

Tradition: This word (from the Latin, meaning "to hand on") in the Catholic Church refers to the process of "handing down" the Gospel. Tradition, which began with the oral communication of the Gospel by the Apostles, was written down in the Scriptures, handed down and lived out in the life of the Church, and interpreted by the Magisterium (the living teaching office) of the Catholic Church, under the guidance of the Holy Spirit.

typology: This word (from the Greek *typos,* meaning "mark" or "figure") refers to a form of biblical interpretation that describes people, events, and symbols of the Old Testament as types, prefiguring people, events, and symbols in the New Testament; for example, the Suffering Servant of the Book of Isaiah is often seen as a type, prefiguring the suffering Jesus. See *senses of the Scriptures.*

Vatican Council II: This ecumenical or general council of the Roman Catholic Church was convoked by Pope John XXIII (1958–1963) and continued under Pope Paul VI (1963–1978). Vatican Council II, which met from 1962 to 1965, provided for an *aggiornamento* (or updating) of Roman Catholic teaching and practice, especially in such areas as liturgy, ministry, religious liberty, ecumenism, and interreligious relations. The Council document *Dogmatic Constitution on Divine Revelation (Dei Verbum)* was instrumental in promoting the reading and studying of the Scriptures that resulted in commentaries and new translations that were accessible to nonscholars.

Vulgate: This word (from the Latin *vulgus,* meaning "common people") refers to the Latin translation of the Bible that was made by Saint Jerome (342–420) from Greek and Hebrew. In 1546, the Council of Trent approved the Vulgate as the authorized text of the Bible for the Roman Catholic Church; subsequent popes have authorized revisions of the Vulgate text.

wisdom: This word (from the Old English "aware" or "cunning") has several meanings: (1) Wisdom is one of the books of the Old Testament; (2) in the Hebrew Scriptures, wisdom is depicted as the action of God in the world; (3) in Christian theology, wisdom is one of the seven gifts of the Holy Spirit and enables a person to know God's divine plan of salvation.

word of God: This term (from the Old English "speech" or "talk") has a variety of meanings: (1) revelation is God's word or message revealed through the prophets in the Old Testament and through Jesus Christ in the New Testament; (2) the Scriptures as the written record of God's communication are the inspired word of God; (3) Jesus as the second person of the Trinity is the embodiment of revelation and the Word of God par excellence.

Yahweh: This word represents the four consonants, usually transcribed YHWH, that were used in the Hebrew Scriptures to indicate the name for God. Modern biblical scholars have reconstructed the word as *Yahweh,* though some have transcribed the Hebrew letters as JHVH and pronounce the name as "Jehovah." The meaning of YHWH is often translated as "I am who I am" (Ex 3:14).

Yahwist: This is a particular school of writing woven throughout the Pentateuch that is attributed to the Yahwist authors or Yahwist school. It is the oldest literary source in the Pentateuch. It is sometimes called the J Tradition because the scholars who first noticed this were German, and in German, Yahweh is spelled *Jahweh.* This J Tradition was probably written by unknown scribes from Judah who in 950 BCE wrote sections of the books of Gen-esis through Numbers. God to the Yahwist had human, or anthropomorphic, qualities. This God walked in the Garden (Gn 3:8), sculpted humanity with divine hands (Gn 2:7), planted groves of trees (Gn 2:8), and grieved at the human beings who were lost among the trees or idols.

Yom Kippur: Yom Kippur is a Jewish holy day that is also referred to as the Day of Atonement, which falls on the tenth day of Tishri and is observed with prayer and fasting in accord with Leviticus (chap. 16).

zealots: This word refers to a Jewish group at the beginning of the first century CE who sought religious and political independence from the Romans and rose up in open rebellion; after their defeat, they carried on guerrilla warfare against the Romans.